CALIFORNIA
INDIAN
COUNTRY

CALIFORNIA INDIAN COUNTRY

The Land & The People

Dolan H. Eargle, Jr.

Trees Company Press
San Francisco

Published by

Trees Company Press
49 Van Buren Way
San Francisco, CA 94131

First printing April, 1992

Library of Congress
Catalog Card: 91-067476
ISBN: 0-937401-20-X (softcover)

Editing:
Lowell Bean • Kathleen Goss
Marie Gobidas

Book Design, Production & Packaging:
Fred Dodsworth & Linda Franklin

Maps:
Mike Mosher

Digital Output:
Tulip Graphics & Publishing, Inc.

Color Separations:
Image Systems

Prepress Services:
Quality Graphics

Printed in the United States:
Times Printing Company, Inc.

Grateful acknowledgement is made to
Frank LaPena for permission to use his
poster Deer Dance Spirit. All other
photographs are by the author.

ACKNOWLEDGEMENTS

Many thanks are due to these people for
assistance, advice, encouragement,
teaching, and information:

Paul Apodaca
Lowell Bean
Chemo Candelaria
Nadyne Gray
Weldon Johnson
Frank LaPena
Malcolm Margolin
Ivadell Mowery
Tom Little Bear Nason
Bev Ortiz
Patricio Orozco
Julia Parker
Lanny and Ester Pinola
Sonne and Elaine Reyna
Jose Ignacio Rivera
Katherine Saubel
Allogan Slagle
Joe Ulmer
Ron Wermuth

...and a great multitude of others
whose names I don't know,
but whose aid has made
this book possible.

TABLE OF CONTENTS

NATIVE CULTURE, PERSISTENCE & TRANSITION

MAPS

A GUIDE TO THE INDIAN PEOPLES OF CALIFORNIA

CENTRAL COAST & CENTRAL VALLEY

(Numbers refer to Map III, page 66)

North of I-80

28   Redding Rancheria

29   Round Valley Reservation

30   Grindstone Creek Rancheria

31   Colusa Rancheria

32   Sherwood Valley Rancheria

33   Potter Valley Rancheria

34   Redwood Valley Rancheria

35   Coyote Valley Rancheria

36   Pinoleville Rancheria

37   Guidiville Rancheria

38   Yo-ka-yo Rancheria

39   Hopland Rancheria

40   Scotts Valley Rancheria

41   Upper Lake Rancheria

42   Robinson Rancheria

43   Big Valley Rancheria

44   El-em (Sulphur Bank) Indian Colony

45   Manchester and Point Arena Rancherias

46   Kashaya (Stewarts Point) Rancheria

47   Cloverdale Rancheria

48   Dry Creek Rancheria

49   Middletown Rancheria

50   Cortina Rancheria

51   Rumsey Rancheria

52   D-Q University

53   Ya-ka-ama (Education Center)

54   Graton Rancheria

South of I-80

55   Kule Loklo (Point Reyes National Seashore)

56   Wilton Rancheria

57   Shingle Springs Rancheria

58   Jackson Rancheria

59   Chaw-Se (Grinding Rocks State Park)

60   Buena Vista Rancheria

61   Sheepranch Rancheria

62   Chicken Ranch Rancheria

63   Tuolumne Rancheria

64   Ahwahnee Village (Yosemite National Park)

65   Wassama Roundhouse (State Park)

66   N. Fork Rancheria & Sierra Mono Museum

67   Picayune Rancheria

68   Big Sandy (Auberry) Rancheria

69   Table Mountain Rancheria

70   Cold Springs Rancheria

71   Santa Rosa Rancheria

72   Indian Canyon

73   Tule River Reservation

EAST OF THE SIERRA DIVIDE

MOJAVE DESERT, COACHELLA VALLEY AND THE COLORADO RIVER

▲ *Tule River Bridge (Tule River Reservation) remains a serviceable relic of a much earlier time.*

PREFACE

THROUGHOUT CALIFORNIA, A REVIVAL OF NATIVE AMERICAN CULTURES IS OCCURRING. Some of these cultures have been dormant for decades, others have been nearly extinguished through suppression and neglect and are now barely emerging from their obscurity, while still others have managed to sustain the practice of their customs and traditions, but only through great tribulations. Somewhat paradoxically, a new, intense interest by the non-Indian community has helped stimulate and encourage the Native cultures to dedicate themselves even more intensely to their own exquisite heritage.

"Indian Country," as used in this book, is a broader term than simply the legal definition of federal trust land or "reservation land." Included here are:

- the many reservation lands, vistas and landscapes in their environs,
- private Native American land owned or rented (meeting centers, schools, anywhere the People congregate),
- more broadly, land which is and has been considered sacred or is of special spiritual significance, even though not located on a reservation (burial grounds, sacred mountains, traditional ceremonial places),
- yet more broadly, older locales of special Indian significance, though not specifically religious (archaeological sites, military forts).

Native American wisdom teaches that the land is a *living* part of creation. With a proper concern for the interactions which permeate all things—the air, the water, the rocks, the creatures, the humans—this creation will survive and all its parts will exist in harmony. If we know the earth, we are prepared to care for it. Therefore, this book is a presentation of that California land of outstanding significance to the Native American heritage, so that all my readers may better know both the Indian land and its people. I have not dwelt upon some topics that could conceivably be approached in such a book as this — employment and income, health, education, nutrition, alcoholism, or clutter. I will leave it to the interested reader to explore these topics, to learn more of the Native people, unless by reading, observing the photos, and visiting the places, it becomes obvious why such problems exist. The people are painfully aware of these problems, and they are doing much to overcome them, even with fewer resources than those provided most of the dominant society.

The California Indians were not architects of kingdoms or massive hierarchies of jade and gold. They were not people of the thundering of horse or bison hooves or of drums. They required not a single fortress or defensive fortification. They were and are people of quiet cultures, very colorful in their own ways, and respectful of the land and their people.

In a world which is increasingly visual in its impact on our senses, I have endeavored to show through recent photographs our Indian Country as it is today; we can see remnants of what has gone before, and grasp a bit of real history. Knowing the past and seeing the world of today, we may better predict what may yet be.

It is to the Native peoples of California that this book is dedicated. May it assist the tribes of all peoples in discovering the California Indian country and the people who are descendants of the first inhabitants of our land. —*Dolan H. Eargle, Jr.*

INTRODUCTION

THE YEAR WAS 1769, SEVEN YEARS BEFORE THE REVOLUTION OF THIRTEEN ENGLISH COLONIES on the East Coast of North America. Somewhere near what is now Tijuana, a group of curious California Indians watched a long, dusty, scraggly procession of pinkish men, some robed, and some mounted and covered with thick leather, accompanied by a rustic band of strange Indians. The long metal tubes carried by the leathered men did not flash with deadly fragments as they had some years before in Mexico, and the long, shiny metal blades swung slowly at their sides unmenacingly. This curious march, filing slowly into California Indian country, did not end until it arrived at San Diego Bay.

California Indian country in 1769 was the entire state — every mountain, river valley, forest, desert and coastal inlet. Only a handful of white men had ever seen the shores of California; in fact, nearly the entire continental United States west of the Mississippi River was mapped as *terra incognita*, a mysterious, unknown land.

Following an urge stimulated by empires with the rapid transport of ships and horses, men with expansionist obsessions spread around the globe, feeding their appetites for curiosity, change, or wealth. They coveted any area that promised to satisfy any of these. Especially attractive were those empires which had already extracted wealth from their own lands, such as Egypt, India, or the American Inca and Aztec nations.

Those were years when mighty empires assumed the right to any lands they could occupy. England had just wrested Canada from France, was suppressing colonial unrest in the American colonies, and was dividing up Louisiana's Indian lands with Spain. California was initially spared this distress, since its richness was not in a form readily seized. But in that year, 1769, the invasion began, the first trickle in a flood that was to inundate much of the Indian population of California within eighty years.

This was the well-supplied group of fifty Spanish soldiers, fifteen monks, and nearly a hundred Mexican Indian "draftees," led by Capitán Gaspar de Portolá and Padre Junípero Serra, who had set out on horseback from Baja California to explore northward into Alta California and to establish missions (run jointly by both church and state) as outposts of the Spanish New World empire. They were supported at sea by three ships of Juan Pérez with whom they rendezvoused six months later at what is now San Diego Bay. Later that year, Portolá explored further north to San Francisco Bay and returned. He had been aiming for Point Reyes via Monterey, somehow missed the latter, and was forced to turn back when he found San Francisco Bay an impasse. His expedition began the cut that was to shred the fabric of the Indian country of California for the next 150 years.

The people the Spanish encountered were like few that they had seen before. The many California tribes more closely resembled small, self-governing independent provinces like those of Baja California than most of the large nations and tribes they had known in central Mexico and in South America. Except for traders, most of the Californians of that early time did not venture far from their homelands; their tribal areas were usually well-defined by the natural topography — mountain ridges, rivers, valleys, edges of deserts, oases, and springs. Since their relative isolation had fostered independence, few groups had felt the necessity for elaborate defense or aggressive warfare. Some groups did have a reputation for conflict over territory and long-lasting family feuds, and the clashes were usually serious when they did occur. However, massive invasions by powerful neighbors were not common, though some displacements have been inferred by linguists. Once the early groups had established their territories, large-scale subjugation of others was not practiced, though some still had a bad reputation for raiding.

They were certainly not well equipped in resisting the mounted, armed, armored, and tactical warfare the Spanish had to offer. The communities had a few combat weapons for their own conflicts — lances and arrows and atlatls[1] for hunting, yes, but not many for sustained warfare against the Spanish. It seems unlikely that this multitude of small, relatively peaceful provinces could have mounted much of a coordinated defense, yet they did for a while, but were unable to maintain it.

At first, many villages welcomed (with reservations) the powerful strangers with curiosity or tried to ignore them; but when the Spanish penchant for crude, rough treatment became intolerable, the Indians revolted strenuously and often effectively. It seems there was always an undercurrent of reaction and rebellion. (See also Mission Era.)

---

[1] atlatl: a notched stick for hurling arrows rather than shooting with a bow.

THE REMOTE PAST
& RECENT PAST

THE EARLIEST PEOPLES OF CALIFORNIA, 12,000 – 2000 B.C.

WHO WERE THESE TRIBES OF ALTA CALIFORNIA, AND HOW HAD THEY COME TO BE HERE? Let us go far back in prehistory, to the time when the great glaciers were melting, the late Pleistocene Age, about 10,000 B.C. California's climate was remarkably different from what it is now. No one had to fight over water rights; the whole state was either wet or frozen, and now-extinct animals roamed the land—camels, tigers, sloths, tiny horses, and huge mammoths. Immense lakes covered land that is desert today. Some spectacular Indian country today is to be found at archaeological and geological sites of the very earliest Indian land.

Cedarville Rancheria and Fort Bidwell Reservation look out on salt lakes that once were fresh-water tributaries to the great ancient Lake Lahontan, which covered eastern California and western Nevada. Two nearby Nevada Paiute reservations are at Pyramid Lake and Walker Lake, other remnants of that great lake. The Timbi-Sha Shoshone Tribe occupies the very bottom of an ancient lake bed in Death Valley. Large parts of the Torres-Martinez Reservation lie flooded under the salty waters of the Salton Sea, a residue of ancient Lake Cahuilla, which covered the Coachella Valley, while other parts border its extinct beaches. Lone Pine Reservation sits at the shores of the former Owens Lake, which dried up because Los Angeles pirated the water. At Calico, near Barstow, once at the wooded shore of ancient Lake Mohave, some early,

unknown tribe ran a factory, shaping thousands of arrows and lances and scrapers for hundreds of years.

About the same time, as early as 5,000 B.C., others of these Early Peoples were making things for living on Santa Rosa Island, off Santa Barbara. There has been much speculation regarding where these early peoples came from — maybe from Asia by boat, maybe across the Bering Strait by a land or ice bridge, and then southeastward, if the ice melted enough to permit passage across Alaska and the Yukon. These are the theories of a race of people from a race who arrived late in California: "We came in late, but we weren't the last. Others must have come in, too, as we did." But these are only theories of persons who are educated in devising theories to fit their facts, and believe in the importance of them. These are not the stories of the Native peoples themselves.

Tribal storytellers can narrate the stories of their origin; moreover, some elders can point out actual places that the stories tell about. The Kawaiisu people of the southern Sierras revere the Coso Hot Springs (located within the China Lake Naval Station), a place where the earth can be heard to continuously rumble and gurgle. Here we are obviously relating to Mother Earth, and her geyser outpourings of vapors and gases vividly demonstrate the powers of creation. The Cahuilla people of the southern California deserts and mountains hold sacred the conical massif of Tahquitz (Tá-kwish), far up on the southwestern summit of San Jacinto Peak (near Idyllwild). This mountain, the tallest in the area, is a spectacular creator of storms, lightning, and thunder.

Not all these places are so awesome. The Konkow story tells of Earth-Initiate (creator), who took a bit of mud and slime from Turtle's fingernails and created Earth. His first landfall was a hillock in the Sacramento River floodplain just south of Chico. The Yurok world center is an unassuming spot along the shore of the Klamath River, just below its confluence with the Trinity River. From such stories of origins, we are made to see the tremendous power of the great spirits in transforming otherwise insignificant places into places of great power. Perhaps the lesson is that no place is truly insignificant.

In the stories of their beginnings, these peoples make no specific reference to time, but do we really need one? Do we need to know the composer and year of a song to appreciate its beauty?

Whatever their origin, the best archaeological evidence shows that around 11 or 12,000 years ago, several bands of very early Indians were making ornate and well designed lance points and arrowheads — finely-shaped like leaves, with fluted center depressions to fit into the arrow shaft. These early works of art have been found at the margins of Borax Lake (Lake Co.) and Tulare Lake (west of Bakersfield), and the Calico site.

More recently (7-6,000 B.C.), people settled in all over the state: from Oroville (Butte Co.) to Lake Mojave (now desert), Death Valley, Diablo Canyon (San Luis Obispo Co. coast), and Topanga Canyon (Los Angeles Co.).

These are the earliest known peoples who settled California Indian country. Some of their artifacts may be seen at the Lakeport Museum (Lake Co.), the Morro Bay State Park Museum, and other, larger archaeological museums of the state. (See Appendix C.)

> FROM SUCH ORIGIN STORIES, WE SEE THE TREMENDOUS POWER OF THE GREAT SPIRITS IN TRANSFORMING INSIGNIFICANT PLACES INTO PLACES OF GREAT POWER.

DEVELOPMENT OF DIFFERENCES

Settling in gave these scattered bands time to develop distinct and unique habits, such as language, religions, lifestyles — *differentiation*, as it is called. The people developed their ways of living by maximizing their relation with the local ecology and by managing the land and the plentiful food sources. It was thus unnecessary to move far from their population centers, their fields and homes. A river valley or plain or marsh or cove was provident enough for whole groups. In these places they evolved new, individual art forms for their beads and basketry and decorative arts. Political structures of society, oral literature, and religious practices grew along with their knowledge of the land.

Clam, abalone, olivella (short, egg-shaped), and dentalium (long, conical) were the most common shells of the California shore, and were useful for trade and money, as well as for personal and artistic ornamentation. The coastal groups were able to trade these hundreds of miles inland for obsidian, the sharpest, strongest, classiest material for arrow and lance points. Obsidian was found only in a few places, such as Mono Lake and Clear Lake, making a good trade item for those tribes fortunate enough to possess it. Elaborate trading networks and trails arose to bring the market goods to the people.

We don't know a lot about the perishable goods (wood, reed, straw, cloth, skins) of the earliest peoples, but we do see from their descendants the art that evolved in their making.

ISLANDS OF HISTORY

The famous Hopi villages, Zuñi, Acoma, Taos, and other Pueblo villages have been inhabited since at least as long ago as 700 A.D. — about the time Paris, France, was settled, and much earlier than for most other European cities. Few people realize, however, that a religious site adjacent to the town of Hoopa in Del Norte County has been in continuous use for nearly 5,000 years. Charcoal dug from the bottom of the fire pit was used to verify this time period by carbon-13 dating.

Though California's Native American cultural heritage was severely damaged by the white incursions, it has by no means been extinguished. The dispersion suffered by numerous tribes in other states was not as drastic here.

Most of the California Natives residing on reservations, and some groups living off-reservation, live within a few miles of their original territories of 1769. Thus, it is not so surprising that the Hupa village site mentioned above is still occupied. Similar instances of continuous, or intermittent, occupation can be found throughout California, though the original buildings are gone. The swirl of the dominant culture has left these places as islands of history.

PATTERNS IN THE FABRIC OF LIFE BEFORE WHITE CONTACT

During the millennia before the white disruption of Native life in California, original tribes apparently underwent a number of displacements before settling down to the established patterns of living. Language similarities are one clue to establishing relationships among various peoples. Language isn't always a reliable clue, since very different peoples may speak related languages, while some closely-related peoples may have almost no common words. Nevertheless, the comparison of the spoken word is still the best indication of closeness.

The color codes in Map I delineate three major languages (called stocks by linguists) in early California: the *Hokan* speakers, found in northern and scattered parts of central and southern California; the *Penutian* speakers, found in a large band running through the central region; and the *Uto-Aztecan* languages, found along the eastern margins, down into the Los Angeles basin and the San Gabriel Mountains. Language experts conclude that the Hokans were the oldest, but were pushed aside or assimilated by a slow drift of Penutian peoples migrating in from the northeast. Then a larger, later migration of Uto-Aztecans flowed in from the Great Basin region, through the Owens Valley. Finally, several *Athapascan*-speaking tribes settled in the northwestern corner of the state, along with a few groups whose language background is indeterminate. It has been estimated that in 1760, California natives spoke more than sixty different languages and dialects, most of which were mutually unintelligible.

Remarkably, there are some thirty California groups today which boast at least one surviving speaker of the old language, and in some, there are persons using the language daily. Recent grants are allowing these valuable persons to be used as resources to record the old languages in stories and accounts of the old times. Moreover, several tribes have established language programs in schools or tribal education programs. Unfortunately, the old languages are being spoken in few homes in Indian California, owing to the pressure of the dominant culture to homogenize all things. Enrichment of our national heritage by preserving ancient languages is not recognized by those who would require only English.

During the early times, a wide-ranging trade network was established to carry goods between the coast and inland. Obsidian, shells, feathers, minerals, salt, fish and other foods, pelts, furs and hides, and bone and antler goods were traded for hundreds of miles distant from their origins. Probably not many individuals actually took long trading trips to these far-off places — that was left up to the multilingual traders with "diplomatic immunity." Some remnants of their trading trails through forest and desert can still be found today. Traders weren't the only ones to influence "intertribal" relations; religious and political leaders of the various regions also established vast networks, enabling the religions to spread and intertribal relations to keep the peace.

As tribes developed, we see the growth of a number of regional religions: the World Renewal, the Kuksu, and the toloache[2]. Of course, each religion had ceremonies, rituals, and occasional gatherings to celebrate their special spirits. As today, these ceremonies of earlier times provided a chance to reaffirm cultural values by reestablishing social and political ties, exchanging goods and gossip, meeting potential mates, and participating in the dances and ceremonies.

The World Renewal, which is found mostly in the northwestern part of the state, is based largely on the seasonal round, especially as marked by the

▲ *Inland salt sources were closely guarded as a great tribal trading asset, as was this Pomo salt spring in Glenn Co., near Stonyford.*

[2] toloache *is the Spanish name for datura, or jimsonweed, a common vine in California with white trumpet-like flowers and large leaves. All parts of this plant are highly hallucinogenic, and fatal in overdose. The early cultures used carefully prepared potions of the plant to sharpen perceptions, to assist dreaming, to gain insights, and occasionally to find lost objects. This is the plant used by the shaman Don Juan in the books by Carlos Castañeda.*

PLACES TO FIND INDIAN ARTWORK

This may be pointing out the obvious, but most older artwork is in museums, and Appendix C is the place to begin looking. Unfortunately, several museums and universities have very large collections that don't allow for public viewing of all the work at any one time (sometimes never!). In a few of these museums there are galleries that sell reproductions of older work, or new work itself. New work can take the form of traditional media and design, as jewelry, woodwork, featherwork, leatherwork, or ceramics. Most important, exceptional modern work by both recognized and newer artists is appearing much more frequently.

Powwows, Big Times, Indian Trade Shows, and Indian Markets are the chance for many, many artists and craftspersons to exhibit their wares. Consult the Events Calendar for some of these events. The reader will probably note that I have not made a great distinction between *art* and *craft*, since there is no fine line to distinguish them. However, painting, printing, and sculpture are fairly separable, I believe. Special galleries run by Native Americans have been opened to show these forms of art; the American Indian Contemporary Arts gallery in downtown San Francisco and Bear 'N Coyote Gallery in Jamestown are two that deserve mention. The American Indian Traders Guild, Inc., of Fresno, is an organization that sponsors trade shows, certifies genuineness of Indian-made goods, and maintains a list of their member traders. (A partial list is to be found in Appendix E.) Some of their authorized traders are not Native American, and some sell only to other shops.

salmon run in the rivers and obvious changes in the seasons. Each year the world is renewed, as provided by the Creator, and the dances celebrate a thanksgiving for this. It is important to distinguish celebration from worship. There are many deities in the Native religions, in the form of spirits who guard our endeavors and foibles. They are honored, not worshipped, and their honoring is a celebration. Among the spirits is usually one which is honored as the most powerful, the creator.

The Kuksu (a powerful spiritual being) and the derivative Bole-Maru have a rather different orientation — originally honoring the persons gone before, but also honoring and celebrating all the spirits that sustain us. Their beautiful and dramatic or representational costumes were conceived "many, many years ago, before the knowledge of anyone alive," by dreamer-shamans. The regalia themselves are danced by the humans, who take upon themselves the spirit, much as do the Pueblo kachina dancers. We find Kuksu ceremonies mainly, but not exclusively, in the tribal groups who have roundhouses, in the central part of the state.

In southern California, one of the powerful spiritual beings is Chi-ngich-ngish. The shamans of this region were often powerful doctors who employed hypnosis, toloache, songs, and ceremonies for curing and mediating with the spirits. In the ceremonies, they were able to transform themselves into animal spirits, when necessary. (A priest or religious authority may also be a shaman, but a shaman is not necessarily a priest.)

The shamans in the south today are generally doctors, and lead ceremonies of healing. Unfortunately, many Native communities have lost many elements of their early religions, owing to their suppression and near eradication by the early missions (more on this later). Nevertheless, the dance, songs, and important ceremonies are being revived in a number of areas; we can expect to see more of them in the near future, as formerly suppressed peoples begin to emerge from their obscurity.

The tribes along the lower Colorado River had yet a different approach to religion. The shaman usually employs a dreaming experience to acquire a spirit helper for the power to cure. He travels in the dream to a sacred mountain, where he encounters a mountain or animal spirit which possesses him to give him the power. Curing is through removal of foreign objects or unhealthy (evil) spirits. Doctoring was powerful, and is to this day.

The vertical scale on this column delineates the year in which the deposits of this Ohlone midden (discard pile) were laid down. It begins in 380 B.C. and tragically ends in 1800, upon displacement by Spanish incursions. The site is in the Coyote Hills Regional Park near Fremont, San Francisco Bay. ▼

TOOLS, FOOD & RELIGIOUS ARTICLES

Those bands of people who were in residence in California during these millennia of 10,000-2,000 B.C., were not big farmers. Archaeologists tell us that the earliest peoples had few seed-grinding tools, so they must have been hunters. We do know that their projectile points and hide-scraping tools were numerous. However, milling stones and grinding rocks began to appear in sites dated around 6,000 B.C. Becoming farmers meant that the bands had to settle down to harvest their crops; we know this from investigations into the numerous *middens*, or garbage piles that these people left. Today, several of these excavated middens can be seen around the state. Of course, the more plentiful the natural resources, the more settlements. Especially densely occupied were sheltered coastal areas of San Diego, Los Angeles, Santa Barbara, San Luis Obispo, and San Francisco, as well as parts of the Central Valley.

For these hunters, the most abundant game appear to have been deer, birds, and fish. In the very earliest times, they probably hunted camel, bison, and horse, but these became extinct, likely due to severe climate changes and to very efficient hunting methods. For similar reasons, we continue to lose species today.

Some time around 3,000 B.C., life became much more diversified in almost all areas of the state. The people were beginning to find many new sources of food and ways to subsist. Some tribes began building elegant fishing boats; others developed complex basketry. In the south, some groups borrowed and adapted pottery and complex techniques for farming corn, beans, and squash (from the nearby Hakataya cultures of Arizona). To sustain this great flowering of unique cultures, the people created whole new sets of constructed things: sharpening stones, cooking and water-carrying baskets, wood carving knives, houses, boats. Life is not just food and shelter: for their spiritual harmony, the people made for themselves magnificently decorated baskets, personal ornaments of bone, shell, and minerals, musical whistles, subtly-executed painted and chipped rock art, and funereal objects that indicate a concern for an afterlife. Associated with this expansion of cultural influences was the rise of a variety of religions (called "cults" by some anthropologists) which were influential over large regions. Many of the patterns of life begun in these times have continued, though attenuated and changed, into the present, as we shall see.

▲ *Modern kids learn to make shell beads using a hand drill.*

▲ *The valley oak produces the acorns for which the grinding rocks at Chaw-se were used. Woodpeckers bore holes in the bark (shown here) in which to "plant" acorns; later, they come back to pick out the weevils which grow in the acorns.*

ROCK ART

For a large, high-visibility, permanent work, an artist will frequently turn to stone. This is especially true where the stone is exposed, smooth, and durable; and granite, sandstone, and some metamorphic rocks of California were particularly well-suited for ancient rock art messages.

Early rock artists used two methods almost exclusively: painting (pictographs) and incision, or "pecking" (petroglyphs: *petro*, rock + *glyph*, carving). Can you imagine a painting or carving that has lasted out-of-doors for nearly a thousand years? Surprisingly, many have; California is fortunate to have the greatest number and variety of ancient rock art examples in the United States.

Paintings that endure for long periods of time need two features, durable painting materials and protection from the elements. Those that we see today have these characteristics—paintings whose colors are amazingly bright. The pigment materials were minerals—carbon (black), iron or mercury oxides (reds), clays (white, yellow, brown), or copper compounds (blue) — while the original binding material must have been of egg or other animal or plant organic matter, long decomposed. Their technology was superb for the task at hand.

The best-preserved paintings, as expected, are found in caves and overhanging rock shelters in almost all parts of the state where such rock features occur. (Unfortunately, the Central Valley is nearly devoid of rock art, owing to the scarcity of such features.)

Petroglyph art was achieved by carefully chiseling with a sharp cutting stone into a rock surface that has a natural polish or "varnish" worn by wind and weather. Thousands of elegant carvings have been found from Lava Beds National Park in the north to the Anza-Borrego Desert in the south.

What messages did the artists want to leave? First of all, we must not consider *any* of these to be idle graffiti; they are serious writings meant to convey information. For instance, some of their meanings[3] might be: trail symbols (a spiral can mean to look up or down for some topographic feature, such as a spring or a shelter), historical (recording of an event, trip, map, story, myth or mythological creature), a religious invocation or homage to a spirit (especially an animal or rain spirit), or a representation of a deity.

All religions use symbols, and a society which devotes itself to the natural world uses many symbols from nature, much as other religions use symbols for worship: the cross or lamb (Christian), the circle (Buddhist), the six-pointed star (Semitic), the

---

[3] *Martineau, Bibliography ref. 14.*

crescent (Islam), the swastika (Hindu, Buddhist, Hopi, Aztec).

Other symbols are facsimiles of or are derived from Indian sign language, which was universally used in North America. Still others are simply artistic decoration.

As Martineau points out, the Native American use of so many symbols for so many purposes should indicate that the North American Indian civilizations were not without a form of writing, contrary to the claims of some anthropologists.

One other form of rock art remains to be mentioned — the intaglios. This form of expression has only a few examples. In eastern Riverside County, huge outlines of figures have been scooped out of the desert stone "pavement." Recent research suggests that these figures were used by Colorado River shamans for symbolic representations of creation stories.

A design similarly made in the desert stone surface is found in Mohave tribal territory near Needles, a maze to confound and divert evil spirits which might try to follow spirits of the dead down the river. Both sites have been partially mutilated by thoughtless persons who lack respect for the heritage of their country.

See Appendix D for a listing of protected archaeological sites of rock art.

▼ *Many petroglyphs, such as these in a natural amphitheater in the Owens Valley, depict symbols of spirits, and with the help of a shaman or priest, invoke their intercession in hunting and weather.*

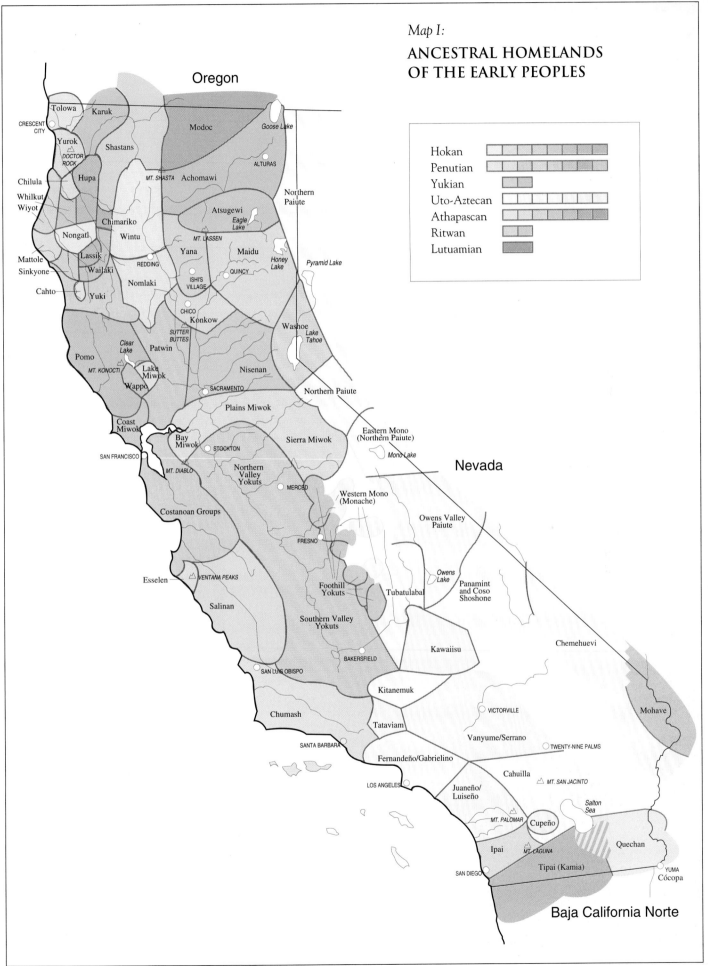

Map I:

ANCESTRAL HOMELANDS
OF THE EARLY PEOPLES

Hokan	
Penutian	
Yukian	
Uto-Aztecan	
Athapascan	
Ritwan	
Lutuamian	

Oregon

Nevada

Baja California Norte

Tolowa
CRESCENT CITY
Karuk
Modoc
Goose Lake
Yurok
DOCTOR ROCK
Shastans
ALTURAS
Chilula
Hupa
MT. SHASTA
Achomawi
Northern Paiute
Whilkut
Wiyot
Chimariko
Atsugewi
Eagle Lake
Nongatl
Wintu
MT. LASSEN
Yana
Maidu
Honey Lake
Mattole
Lassik
REDDING
QUINCY
Pyramid Lake
Sinkyone
Wailaki
Nomlaki
ISHI'S VILLAGE
Cahto
Yuki
CHICO
Konkow
Washoe
Lake Tahoe
SUTTER BUTTES
Clear Lake
Patwin
Pomo
MT. KONOCTI
Lake Miwok
Nisenan
Wappo
SACRAMENTO
Coast Miwok
Plains Miwok
Northern Paiute
Bay Miwok
STOCKTON
Sierra Miwok
Eastern Mono (Northern Paiute)
SAN FRANCISCO
MT. DIABLO
Mono Lake
Northern Valley Yokuts
MERCED
Western Mono (Monache)
Owens Valley Paiute
Costanoan Groups
FRESNO
Owens Lake
Panamint and Coso Shoshone
Esselen
VENTANA PEAKS
Foothill Yokuts
Tubatulabal
Salinan
Southern Valley Yokuts
Chemehuevi
SAN LUIS OBISPO
Kawaiisu
BAKERSFIELD
Kitanemuk
Mohave
Chumash
Tataviam
Vanyume/Serrano
SANTA BARBARA
VICTORVILLE
Fernandeño/Gabrielino
TWENTY-NINE PALMS
LOS ANGELES
Cahuilla
Juaneño/Luiseño
MT. SAN JACINTO
Salton Sea
MT. PALOMAR
Cupeño
Ipai
MT. LAGUNA
Quechan
Tipai (Kamia)
YUMA
SAN DIEGO
Cócopa

THE OLDEST STRUCTURES

▲ *At Satwiwa (in the Santa Monica Mountains), both Chumash and Gabrielino peoples have erected frameworks for reconstruction of large traditional reed-covered dwellings. Boney Mountain, an unusual nature refuge, stands in the distance.*

▲ *The year-round warmth of the lower Colorado River Valley demanded that the natives of the area build cool, shading structures like this clay-covered sapling house adjacent to the Ft. Yuma Reservation Museum.*

In northwestern California, where winds, rain, and fog make indoor living preferable much of the year, the early peoples built reasonably permanent structures resembling a sunken garage with a crown and a small round door to discourage bears. Patio stones were even used to pave around the doorway. The living area inside was split-level with a shelf-deck around the walls wide enough for sleeping and for storage, while the cooking and chores were done in a depressed area in the center. Several of these buildings can be visited today — **Yurok** homes at Sumeg, **Hupa** dwellings at several sites on the reservation near the town of Hoopa. The community structures were similar — one restored building used for religious purposes occupies a site that is some 5,000 years old!

Sumeg Yurok Village is located at Patricks Point State Park on U.S. 101 in Humboldt Co. Structures include four smaller dwellings, one large home, a sweathouse, and a covered dance pit.

Djistanadin is the site of one of several ancient villages on the **Hoopa Reservation**, near the airport. Several very old houses and a dance "pit" are found in the village.

Further south, central California tribes often used a form of cedar tipi — a large conical semi-permanent structure. Other peoples built a round, slightly sunken, rock-lined house, covered with mud or long strips of cedar or redwood bark. Examples of the former can be seen at **Chaw-Se**, **Wassama** (the town of Ahwahnee), **Ahwahnee Village** (Yosemite Park), and **North Fork Mono Museum**.

In the desert areas, the most popular shelter was made of reed or woven sapling-branches; these were open in the hot places, close-woven in the high, cooler places. Woven reed was the material of choice in the southeastern region, also, while surprisingly large tule reed houses were used in the **Chumash** and neighboring **Fernandeño** and **Gabrielino** areas. Smaller reconstructions of the reed homes may be seen in the **Los Angeles Museum of Natural History** and the yard adjacent to the **Santa Ynez Reservation** clinic. A reconstruction of the early wattle-and-daub (mud over sapling branches) homes of the Colorado River **Quechan** people is alongside the **Ft. Yuma Reservation Museum**.

By far the most elaborate structures built by the California Indian peoples are the dancehouses or roundhouses. From the northern Sacramento River valley, along the Coast Range and the Central Valley to the southern Sierras, these traditional centers have been erected for tribal religious rites. But they are not just "churches." On reservations they serve as a place for meetings, making important decisions, serving shared meals, socials, instruction, and singing, as well as the sacred tribal rites — all under the guidance of the spirits. Each roundhouse differs in its tribal specifications, but the importance of the place calls for careful design dictated by tradition. Participation in a roundhouse ceremony is a particular and very special privilege. (See Appendix D for a listing.)

▲ *Indian residents of Yosemite Park demonstrate the usefulness of the Sierra Miwok bark slab tipis in the Visitor Center Village. These tipis are used today by Native Americans visiting Indian dance gatherings.*

▶ *Reconstruction of traditional gabled Hoopa plank house at Djistandin, near the town of Hoopa.*

▲ *Aerial view of the diorama at the Peralta Adobe City Park (San José). The adobe itself, still standing, was built with Ohlone labor.*

THE CLASH OF NATIVE VERSUS EUROPEAN

EFFECTS OF THE FIRST CONTACTS

For 200 years before the fateful Spanish invasion in 1769, the Native population of Alta California had been paid only sporadic visits by European sailors, many of whom were rather rude to their hosts. The first, repairing his damaged boat near Point Reyes, was Sir Francis Drake (1579), followed by Sebastian Vizcaino (1602) and Juan de Oñate (1604). Other Spanish, English, and French ships put in for provisions, but the arrogant behavior of most crews gave the white man a deservedly bad reputation. Russian sailors seem to have been the only crews that treated the Indians with some respect.

Toward the end of this two-century era, the Quechan of southeastern California were already being stricken by European disease, transmitted westward from the Spanish occupation of Pueblo country. In eastern California, Paiutes were raided in 1609 by Ute cousins from further east, who captured slaves to sell to New Mexican Spanish. Agriculture and dietary customs were rapidly upset by the introduction of wheat, replacing corn and beans, in the Colorado River area around 1700. The horse came into use in eastern areas, although in many tribes it served mainly as food.

It was into this milieu that Spanish authorities in Mexico dispatched Padre Fray Junípero Serra and his company to save souls, to explore, to claim the land for Spain, and to try to discourage Russian and English expansion.

EUROPEAN SETTLEMENT, RIPS IN THE THREAD
Spanish: 1769-1825, Mexican: 1825-1846

Over a period of only fifty-six years, the Spanish invasion and colonization provoked an almost total rending of the Native fabric of the southern coastal half of California. With 250 years of experience in cultural extermination in the heart of Mexico, the Spanish occupiers began to apply their methods northward. The padres would approach a village, in a place that appeared to be reasonably self-sustaining with water, food supply, and a fair-sized population. Their reception varied from a curious welcoming to frigid to hostile. A few natives, seeking to possess some of these strangers' "power," allowed themselves to be baptized. After dedicating the place (for instance, the Serra landing site in Monterey), the padre would spend a short time in residence, then move on, leaving the chore of actually building a mission to his subordinates.

The hard labor of adobe and stonemasonry, earth moving, Spanish-style farming, and heavy tasks was done by "neophytes," newly-converted Natives, who zealously took to their assigned tasks, voluntarily at first, then under the prodding of the soldiers. Under the rules of the Church of Rome, a harsh new regime replaced the less structured village life of the people. They were usually compelled to live within the mission compound, segregated by sex, restrained from much of their earlier life styles, forbidden to use their language, religion, and dances. They were told what new foods to eat, and roughly commanded to raise wheat, weave, make olive oil and wine for officials in Mexico. In some places, San Gabriel and San Francisco, for instance, dances were permitted for a few years, but were eventually prohibited. Also at San Gabriel, use of the language was permitted in some villages which had been allowed to continue.

The Native Californian was soon not overly impressed with the joys promised by the padres. Nearly every mission experienced at least one major rebellion over these 50 years. Indeed, in 1781, the Quechans of Yuma, to show their great displeasure at having Spanish cattle devour their food and having their trade routes disrupted, killed the padre, threw out the army, and remained independent until overpowered by American army forces decades later.

Throughout the history of Europe, the Middle East, Africa, and Asia, disease had swept the populations, often reducing towns to one-third of their former size. Such epidemics had left these people with a fairly strong genetic immunity to many afflictions. Nevertheless, they carried the germs of these terrible plagues with them when they arrived in the Western Hemisphere. Whatever other societal treatment the Native Californians were offered, they were helpless before the onslaught of these new diseases. Once the people were forced into mission compounds, not even modern medicine could have prevented the epidemics that followed. It is astounding that the padres were so calloused to the havoc they were causing, as, when their labor force became depleted, they called upon the soldiers to range ever wider in their search for able-bodied workers.

Rebellion or flight prompted stern measures from the Church — imprisonment, deportation to other missions, lashing, chopping off of toes; escapees risked death, if caught. Luís Peralta, Gervásio Argüello, and Father L.A. Martinez, Spaniards commemorated in California place names, were noted for their enthusiasm in gathering in "apostates." They were known to brag about their entrapment or killing of fugitives.

Life in the missions was not always as idyllic as some of the propaganda tells. Of the 56,000 Indians baptized during this period, only 15,000 lived beyond 1834. The specter of death was everpresent; the thought of flight suppressed. Still, many did flee — into the unknown world outside and with threat of severe punishment if caught.

Perhaps life could have been fairly normal for those who adjusted to the new ways, or had been permitted to live in the countryside villages, adjacent to some missions in the south. Nevertheless, the missions were built with four walls for a reason — which was not to keep people *out*.

The last few years of this period saw some changes in the Indian condition, for in 1821, Mexico became independent of Spain, with California becoming a *Territorio* of Mexico four years later. The official position of the Mexican government swung in favor of the condition of the people. Some Indians were now permitted to leave the missions to become independent agents for the Spanish immigrants of the new towns, the *pueblos*.

THE MISSIONS WERE BUILT WITH FOUR WALLS, NOT TO KEEP PEOPLE OUT. REBELLION OR FLIGHT PROMPTED STERN MEASURES: IMPRISONMENT, DEPORTATION TO OTHER MISSIONS, LASHING, CHOPPING OFF OF TOES, EVEN DEATH.

In the countryside, the *hacienda* or *rancho* became the dominant way of life, employing the Indian as *peon* or *vaquero*, especially after the decline of the power of the missions. In 1834, the Mexican government "secularized" (i.e., nationalized) the missions, freeing the Indians from serfdom. Most fled from the system, though converted to Christianity, and the mission system crumbled. The Mexican government had intended that most of the huge landholdings of the missions would go to Indian owners, the very people who had suffered and worked the lands for so many years.

But the real owners turned out to be the former Spanish *Californios* who had taken power and land. These rancheros,

▲ *Foreboding carvings watch over the Campo Santo (burial grounds) of Mission Santa Barbara. Several thousand Chumash are interred here.*

▲ *Gen. Mariano Vallejo forced Wappo and Suisun Patwin Indians to build his huge Rancho Petaluma in Sonoma Co. This building served as residence, shops, barns, and rancho headquarters.*

THE MISSION ERA, A TIME OF STRAIGHT LINES

With the coming of the Spanish from central Mexico, a new and very different set of architectural visions was introduced. The California Indians were accustomed to artistic expression in a free form — structures and artistic objects blended with nature and allowed the eye to join the object with irregularities of trees and stone. The padres and Spanish had other ideas — to make a building stand out from the countryside.

Made of adobe bricks and shaped stone, the walls, dwellings, churches, and auxiliary buildings took the form of straight lines, sharp angles, and studied arches. They all demand to be seen. Within and without the buildings and their arcades, lines converge to near infinity. The Indian way of life had been open and free, using temporal thin or open reed structures. But once the Spanish imposed a more sedentary life upon the Native people, they adopted and adapted the use of adobe over most of southern California. It was available, cheap, and comfortable. A few old adobe homes and structures are still in use today, modified and modernized, especially on the **La Jolla** and **Pauma** reservations.

The adobe techniques were used to full advantage by the *rancheros*, the well-to-do Spanish who came to California to settle. Several of their elegant homes, built with Indian labor, survive.

For the mission churches, cloisters, compounds, and their complex waterworks, elaborate stonework was used. During this era, a number of Indians became distinguished as stonecarvers, creating fountains, columns, statues, and other stone artwork, but never in their own tradition, rather in the tradition of old Mexico, derived from the Italian. We must never forget that these romantic, beautiful buildings were constructed entirely with Indian labor; the tribes are so recognized in Appendix B.

such as Pio Pico, Sebastian Peralta, and José Sepúlveda, were joined by a number of other Europeans and Americans who adopted Mexican citizenship, such as Juan Warner and Johann Sutter. The owners of these extensive lands founded extremely powerful families, whose influence has lasted to the present day. The ranchos, themselves, however, did not long survive the invasion of the American horde, whose greed for gold, and later for land, outweighed their concern for Indian or ranchero.

LIFE BEYOND THE MISSIONS, SNAGS IN THE WEAVE

The effect of the mission on Indian life in the state was, of course, most pronounced depending on a group's proximity to the mission. Yet, utilizing the elaborate Indian trading networks, a demand for Spanish metals, tools, and goods was growing. Also growing was the spread of imported disease.

Northern California was the section of the state least affected by the Spanish invasion, being the most distant and the most remote. Indeed, the northernmost missions were not established until in the early 1800s, and had little time to penetrate the life of the northern peoples. But at the same time, rancheros such as Mariano Vallejo and Luís Peralta were moving in on the best land, spreading tyranny and disease.

Most northern California tribes did manage to evade the worst epidemics until the American invasion, but decimation of the Central Valley tribes was inevitable. In ever-widening waves the rancheros went in search of laborers, kidnapping and condemning to serfdom

those Indians they could catch. Johann Sutter and Mariano Vallejo (and sons) were among the most notorious for establishing Indian mercenary armies to subdue nearby tribes. When they could, the Natives employed guerilla tactics to defend their lands. Estánislao (Stanislaus) escaped Missión San José, organized a band of resistance fighters in the Central Valley, defeated his Mexican army pursuers in 1829, and fought on until 1838.

In southern California, those tribes to the east were the least affected, though they were subjected to secondary pressures from the Spanish occupation of Arizona and New Mexico— migration and raids by Ute and Paiute refugees pushed westward. The Kamia and, to some extent, the Cahuilla of the South Coast Range managed to stay independent through stiff resistance and clever avoidance of pitched battles with Spanish troops. Not until the American influx were they completely overcome. The Colorado River tribes, too, stayed relatively independent, though severely annoyed by Spanish settlement on their east in Arizona and south in Mexico.

THE STAGE WAS SET FOR THE DRAMA THAT WAS TO TEAR APART THE FABRIC OF THE OLD WAYS. AMERICAN MANIFEST DESTINY, THE MARCH TO THE WESTERN SEA, WAS ABOUT TO BEGIN.

One reflection must be offered about this period. Although the Spanish attitude towards the Indian was often patronizing and excessively stern, it at least recognized the Native as human and deserving of certain rights. This approach differed markedly from that of the incoming American, whose attitude could only be described as *bad*. The average American immigrant thought of the Indian as something approaching that of a pest to be exterminated, or at best, to be put to use as forced labor. It took over 75 years to overcome this sentiment.

Arcades of four missions. Spanish architecture, with its rectangular, linear concept, contrasted sharply with that of the indigenous concept of harmonizing with the irregularities of nature.

Top Left: Santa Ynez (Santa Barbara Co.),

Top Right: San António de Pádua (Monterey Co.),

Bottom Left: Purísima Concepción (Lompoc, Santa Barbara Co.),

Bottom Right: San Juan Capistrano (Orange Co.)

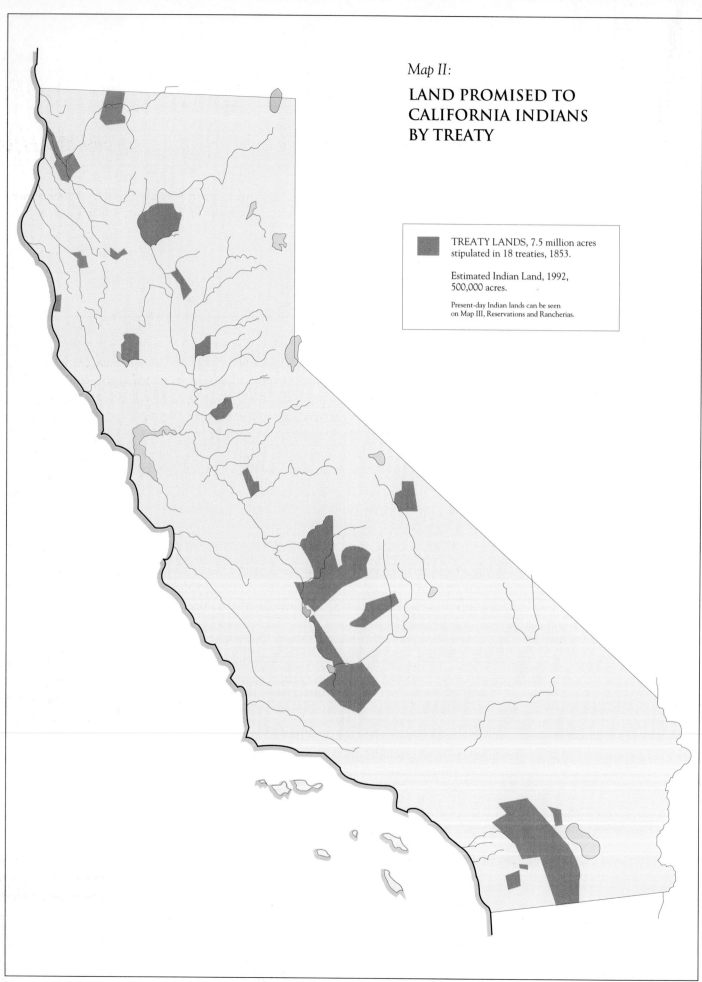

Map II:

LAND PROMISED TO CALIFORNIA INDIANS BY TREATY

TREATY LANDS, 7.5 million acres stipulated in 18 treaties, 1853.

Estimated Indian Land, 1992, 500,000 acres.

Present-day Indian lands can be seen on Map III, Reservations and Rancherias.

THE AMERICAN INVASION, SHREDDING THE FABRIC

On a dry and dusty day in 1841, the first American immigrant train, the Bidwell-Bartleson company, clattered into Mexican Alta California. Already, for thirty years American sailboat skippers had been assisting coastal pueblos in a way that Spain and Mexico could not — trading for essential supplies. The stage was being set for the drama that was to tear apart the fabric of the old ways of life. American Manifest Destiny — the march to the western sea — was about to begin in California.

On the pretense of scientific surveys in 1844 and a more blatant military operation in 1846, Capt. John C. Frémont freely roamed central California, eventually raising the American flag on a hill near Gilroy. Along with American forces from Santa Fe under General Stephen Kearny, and naval Commodores Robert Stockton and John Sloat, Frémont forced the Mexican Army to capitulate in 1847. Alta California was ceded to the U.S. by the Treaty of Guadalupe Hidalgo on February 2, 1848. A few days before, at a sawmill owned by Johann Sutter, a Swiss entrepreneur who had founded a small empire at Sacramento, a New Jersey wagon builder found a small gold nugget. Gold fever, among other fevers, ran rampant, and the mass American immigration began.

The white immigrants arrived with a frenzied greed for gold or land, bringing with them an enthusiasm that also infected Afro, Asian, and Indian. Most of the white horde came from poverty in the East or from the slavery culture of the South, passing through Midwestern lands occupied by a thoroughly hostile Indian population. They were in no mood for such distractions as "primitive" Indians who protested the seizure and spoilage of their lands and homes. Though a few were drafted as laborers, the Indian was pushed aside and ignored, and if there was protest, punished by the sternest measures, including extermination.

By 1854, the gold supply was dwindling rapidly, the best lands having been taken or depleted. A general financial depression settled upon the pioneers. There was work to be sought, crooks and ruffians to be dealt with, land and survival to be considered, and soon, a Civil War to be fought. There was no time for any interference.

CALIFORNIA STATEHOOD

It was 1850, and California was admitted to the Union as a "free" state — an appellation that didn't seem to extend to the Indian population. Until mid-century the eastern United States had a policy of Indian "removal" further and further west, but this policy could hardly be used anymore. Certainly something had to be done with the Native Californians, but what? In 1851 a delegation of three commissioners was sent from Washington to make "peace" treaties with the tribes — the treaties to consist of removing the Indians to reservations in order to reduce Indian-white friction and to maintain a ready supply of cheap labor nearby. Treaties were actually negotiated with eighteen groups (not tribes), promising teachers, farm advisers and implements, blacksmiths, seed, and cloth, and 7.5 million acres of reservation lands (see Map II) in exchange for the relinquishment of claim to most of the state. The Natives began to honor their part of the "signed" treaties, withdrawing to the designated lands and refraining from armed conflict. Congress, however, refused to acknowledge the treaties and the responsibilities in them, under pressure from greedy California legislators.

Nevertheless, a number of larger reservations were established between 1853 and 1887, the majority of them either in uninhabitable locations, or in climates totally unsuitable for the inhabitants. Of the original ten reservations, parts of

SOME NUMBERS

In 1845, the Mexican population of Alta California was 4,000. In 1847, the Americans numbered 15,000; in 1850, they were 93,000; in 1860, 380,000. On the other hand, estimates of the Native population in 1776 range from at least 300,000 to an easily-sustained one million. (Estimates, then or now, for heavily-populated areas, such as San Francisco, San Diego, and Los Angeles are impossible to fix.)

By 1850, the Indian populations, already severely affected by the massive influx of disease, could no longer resist the swamping of their cultures.

five remain. Over the next 75 years, a large number of rancherias (small residential villages) were established, often on or near the original tribal lands, by executive order or Congressional bill, but total reservation lands never exceeded 500,000 acres.

GENOCIDE

Where disease had not exterminated the Indian populations, the next sixty years brought mutilation of their cultures. The reader may judge — I will extract some accounts from "The Earth Is Our Mother"[4]:

What resistance the Indians could muster to the depletion of their food sources and the threat of starvation took the form of drawing upon the white man's resources — stealing cattle, food, and dwelling supplies. This, in turn, aroused reprisal and vengeance far in excess of the "injury" done. Occasionally, the Indian would react violently and the vicious cycle was on.

The Army was called upon to "protect and restrain" the Indians. "Protection" was minimal, and "restraint" was usually pursuit. Nearly 200 military forts and posts were erected in California for control of the Indians, some directly on the reservations. The military's "protection" did little good in altering the public's attitude toward Indians.

Allow me to recount some incidents of Indian persecution in this period:

• Two settlers, Charles Stone and Andrew Kelsey, oppressed Clear Lake Pomos held in serfdom on their rancho to the point of lashing, rape, slavery, and murder. Incensed by this treatment, Stone and Kelsey were executed by two natives enraged by this inhuman treatment. The other Indians, fearing certain reprisal, fled to an island at the north end of the lake. But the Army was called out to dispense vengeance, brought boats, and massacred 60 of the 400 on the island, now called "Bloody Island." Women and especially children were easy prey. Pursuit took another 75

Indian lives, including some "hanged and burnt." A Treaty of Peace and Friendship followed, in which the Pomo relinquished their lands for a gift of "10 head of beef, three sacks of bread, and sundry clothing." (1850-51, Lake Co.)

• At a feast given by whites for 300 Wintu, all Indians present were ambushed one-by-one by soldiers and volunteers. (1850s, Shasta Co.)

• Nearly 100 Yuma and Mohaves were drowned in an alkali lake in retaliation for raids on cattle and immigrant trains. (1865, Inyo Co.)

• On the Trinity River, some Hupa were displaced by white settlers. Upon returning to fish their waters, they were shot. (1855, Humboldt Co.)

• General Kibbe reported a policy to drive the Achumawi into the mountains to starve during food-gathering seasons. (1850, Siskiyou Co.)

• Accounts from Humboldt and Trinity counties report many of the worst depredations – nearly 50 rancherias and encampments attacked, burned, ambushed, the inhabitants slaughtered. (1855-63)

• Survivors of three Eel River tribes were encamped on Indian Island in Humboldt Bay, Eureka, attempting to avoid white contact. While the men were away fishing, the local whites descended upon the women, children, and elderly, literally butchering them all. (Author Bret Harte denounced the raid in print, and was fired from his journalist post.) (1860, Humboldt Co.)

• In retaliation for attacking an immigrant train, a detail of 58 dragoons and infantry killed 20 Indians near Ft. Mojave, then retreated to San Bernardino (1858). The Army returned and took the land without bloodshed, by taking six chieftains hostage. Hostilities again erupted, with the Army killing 23 Mohaves and destroying their crops. (1859, San Bernardino Co.)

• Scattered inhabitants of the

◄ *Indian Island in Humboldt Bay (Eureka), is the site of a hideous massacre of Wiyot and Eel River tribes in 1860.*

[4] (Ref. 4, et al.): *These accounts are drawn from Cook (1976), Forbes (1965), Heizer (1978), and Rawls (1984), all of which detail other tragedies.*

▲ *An adobe building at Ft. Tejon, to which hundreds of Indians from several tribes living in the Tehachapi and southern Sierra mountains were rounded up and brought in 1854. This camp was totally inadequate for habitation by more than a few persons — no food, shelter, nor means of subsistence. It was abandoned in 1864.*

Tehachapi Mountain Range of Ventura, Los Angeles, Kern, and Santa Barbara counties were rounded up and marched to Ft. Tejon. (1853)

• Achumawi and Maidu of the northeast were driven hundreds of miles to Round Valley. (1860, Mendocino Co.)

• A roundup of the Sacramento Valley drove peoples to the Nome Lackee Reservation. (1863, Tehama Co.)

• Cupeños were removed from Warner Springs to Pala. (1903, San Diego Co.)

• "Trails of Tears" – long, forced marches of the weary and bedraggled remnants of once-happy peoples, removed from their homes to reservations that were worthless spots of land bereft of any food or shelter.

Disease, the unseen decimator, took its horrible toll:

• One hundred of nearly 500 villagers near Yuba City died of cholera. (1849, Yuba Co.)

• At one of Sutter's farms, 40 of 48 died of an epidemic. The next year 500 died. (1852, Placer Co.)

Short-lived and sporadic resistance by Indians arose in several places, no contest ending in Indian success.

Juan Antonio Garrá, a Cupeño, organized a successful revolt of several southern California desert peoples. The Colorado River and parts of the Mojave came under Indian control, but the movement collapsed when Garrá was betrayed by disloyal Indians. The Army destroyed the food supplies of the involved peoples in retaliation. Garrá was executed, and the chief Cupeño village was burned. (1851-52, San Diego, Imperial, Riverside Cos.)

There was hardly a group that did not defy the intruders. The more well-known conflicts between the settled natives and the army have been recorded: Hamakhavas (Mohaves) (1850-1860s), Owens Valley Paiutes (1850s-1865),

Klamath War (1851-52), Shoshones (1850s-1865), Northern Paiutes (1860s), Kern River War (1856), Pit River "Massacres," (1867), Modoc War (1872-73).

Some reservations proved to be essentially concentration camps. The miserable inhabitants fell victim to fraud, appropriation of supplies, maltreatment, and gross neglect by camp administrators. The Army's guarantee of protection often proved worthless. In 1862, 45 Indians of Round Valley were murdered *in camp* by neighboring whites; a year later 20 Wailaki were murdered in the same place. The only defense was to flee, but where?

Some persons disappeared into the most remote areas. In familiar territory, some banded together gypsy-like in camps living at the rural edge of white society. Others took refuge with settled Indian groups, still others were befriended by whites or ranchers. Quite a few were obliged to deny their Indianness and passed as "Mexican" or African-American. Southern California fared somewhat better than further north during this period. Here, there was far less gold, consequently less American interference; the Native peoples had already suffered and survived the major scourge of disease. In the coastal Mission areas, the Church served in some degree to integrate the Indians into society; and outside the Mission areas, strong tribal unity aided in sustaining many cultural aspects. The census of 1900 reported only some 16,000 Native Americans, though it is known that many thousands of Natives wisely chose not to be recognized. (Many still do not choose this recognition.)

Only the barest threads of the original culture remained, but a restoration of some of the fabric was possible. 🔫

Counting – Modoc Petroglyphs, Lava Beds N.P.

◀ *A cactus blooms at the ruins of Ft. Paiute, site of a desert spring (eastern San Bernardino Co.) appropriated by the Army from the Paiutes in its campaign to establish a wagon trail across the southern California desert.*

A TIME OF ENDURANCE AND RESTORATION

Some outcast peoples of this world possess a power and will to survive to survive. Though incredibly beleaguered, decimated, dispersed, and alone, the Native peoples of California found themselves faced with this challenge, and very slowly, this power began to reveal itself.

One first need is shelter — building from available materials, from discarded lumber or adobe. Another first need is food — planting or harvesting native plants in a manner based on what one remembers from earlier times, or adapting newly-introduced seeds and plants. Another need is health — very difficult to maintain in a land where the healthful food and medicinal herbs were devastated. Another need is a stubborn faith in what is right. Somehow, the people found these things.

When one is concerned with the basics of survival, issues of human rights seldom appear important. The rights of Indians had been extinguished — no private property, no recourse to the justice system, no vote, no education. National attention slowly was attracted to Indian problems with the help of some widely-publicized court battles (e.g., Helen Hunt Jackson). These rights were not recovered until the 20th century — voting rights were not established until 1924; with the vote came the others, granted only grudgingly.

Land in the form of small rancherias has been acquired by Presidential and Congressional acts through the past 75 years, but even this miserly generosity has sometimes been reversed in strangely contradictory governmental behavior. In the 1950s, Congress sought to elimi-nate some "Indian problems" simply by eliminating Indian land and requiring Indians to "assimilate." Several rancherias were illegally "terminated" from "trust" status through this process. Fortunately, most have been partially restored, but some land was irrevocably lost. Within the last decade, several additions to Indian land have been purchased for housing by the Department of Housing and Urban Development and the Bureau of Indian Affairs. Major additions have also been donated by the Bureau of Land Management, which seems delighted to return some of its land to the original owners. All government landholders should be encouraged to do the same.

Indian education has gone through some bizarre changes during the last 100 years. Serious efforts at providing Indian schooling were not begun by either state or local authorities until the turn of the century. Some larger reservations provided day schools or boarding schools, but many of these closed, owing to heavy absenteeism. For decades, large numbers of Indian students were affected by rampant epidemics, more so than the white population.

Many times, Indian parents perceiving the insidious destruction of their cultures, withdrew their children from schools which were cruel, military-style racist institutions. Pupils were forcibly prevented from using their language or customs, while removed long distances from their parents.

For a time in the last century, federal authorities tried a new tack — Christian church administration of the reservations. Their schools, too, often turned

> ## THE BAREST THREADS OF THE ORIGINAL CULTURE REMAINED, BUT A RESTORATION OF SOME OF THE FABRIC WAS POSSIBLE.

SONG OF THE FISH CRANE

*Fish Crane with
your beautiful flowery feathers,*

*Fish Crane with
your beautiful flowery feathers,*

*I wish I could fly
as you can fly.*

Wukchumni Yokuts song from Tawish Sabagi (Leon Manuel) in Songs of the Yokuts and Paiutes, *A. Pietroforte, Naturegraph Press, Happy Camp, CA, 1965.*

◀ *Spring flowers in the rocks of Pa-che-pus (Esselen, Monterey Co.), high in the mountains of Big Sur.*

ARCHITECTURE AT THE TURNING OF THE CENTURY

With the American influx came the miners, mostly from the poorer parts of the Eastern United States. Knowing their tenure would be very short, they lived in extremely primitive conditions, but so did the Indians they displaced, who were at the very least trying to survive, and possibly to raise families. The style of dwelling the miners raised were what they had known, log cabins and wooden clapboard shacks. Owing to the ready availability of the materials, Indians copied the style, especially toward the end of the century, when life had settled down somewhat. Some of these simple turn-of-the-century dwellings, built in nearly every California Indian community, are extant and even occupied, though modified somewhat. A few examples should be preserved for their historical value, that Indian and non-Indian alike not forget the conditions of living not so long ago.

At this time in history, the many Christian churches also made their unique impression on the California Indian countryside. Their architecture was generally copied from that of the nearby towns, which in turn was derived from that of the Eastern United States, whence they had arisen. Consequently, in the far northwest we find a tidy Shaker church on the **Smith River Rancheria**, a one-room rectangular Pentacostal worship hall on the **Bishop Reservation**, lovely one-room clapboard Catholic chapels at the reservations **in Jamul** and **Sycuan**, and an unusual old Moravian church on the **Morongo Reservation.**

out to be cruelly run and corrupt, and once again Indian cultural values were suppressed. Nevertheless, missionaries have continued to be allowed upon the reservations and have introduced schooling of their own.

Eventually, students seeking secondary education, albeit in the values of the dominant society, were offered the Indian School in Carlisle, Pennsylvania or **Sherman Indian High School**, a boarding school in Riverside, California. (For a description of its history, see p. 126.) Indian secondary education for California students is also available at the private school in Pala, and at Stewart School in Carson City, Nevada.

Even today, only the largest reservations have their own schools; elsewhere, pupils attend local schools. Instruction in tribal and cultural history and customs remains a task for the tribe itself, sometimes on a released-time basis. **D-Q University** near Davis, California's only Native American institution of higher education, offers courses in social sciences, the sciences and humanities, and agriculture. Its approach to course offerings in indigenous studies are uniquely Native American, though some Native American studies programs are to be found at campuses of the University of California and California State Universities. Several community colleges have begun offering courses with a Native American-California orientation. Hopefully, California's Native cultural heritage can be restored.

Only within the last decade has Indian health received adequate attention in California. The impoverished peoples of the preceding 100 years had to find medical and health care where they could. At first, public health programs in the Indian communities were as expected — nil. The people had to rely on

their traditional herbal and shamanic medicine, which too often were ineffective against the European-introduced epidemics. The Indian doctors tried, and when they failed, lost the peoples' confidence.

It was not until 1901 that the Indian people had a hospital, at Sherman School in Riverside. One can well imagine what health was in the distant rural areas. Since the 1970s, the Indian Health Service has been trying to establish clinics in all the major areas of need, so that several of the more rural reservations and rancherias now have at least an itinerant doctor, nurse, dentist, and oculist. Modern Indian clinics are located in Bishop, Burney, Fort Bidwell, Ft. Yuma, Morongo, Round Valley, Trinidad, Tule River, and Tuolumne, among others. Other communities, including urban Indian groups, must find health care within their local public health system. Outpatients to these clinics are offered help with maternity care, nutrition, alcoholism, and AIDS. As in most programs, stingy, nearsighted budgeteers offer the least to those most in need.

INDIAN POWER?

Heroes are those who struggle against intimidating odds. Many known (such as Billy Beckwith, *Hupa*, and Francisca Patencio, *Cahuilla*) and many more unnamed Indian heroes arose during the painful times of recovery — those who protested the extermination of people and culture, those who demanded rights, those who wanted only justice for their people. At times of great necessity, the people organized in regional groups over and over, and still they emerge when needed.

Then came the heroes of anti-bureau-

> ENTHUSIASM IS EVERYWHERE. IN ALL PARTS OF THE STATE, CULTURES ARE EMERGING FROM A QUIET AND PRIVATE EXISTENCE TO A MORE PUBLIC ONE.

cracy. Lately have come those who can badger and manipulate the bureaucracy and cut the white tape for the betterment of their people.

The Indian people of California have shown their will to survive, to grow, to perpetuate their heritage and to demonstrate it to all the world, whether that world watches or not. The work is not yet done, but it is easier. The hearts and minds of *all* the people are not yet won. The difficulties of the future will not be the burdens of the past — they will be the difficulties of stimulating enthusiasm among the young, of maintaining the continuity, the thread of the ageless and reweaving it into the fabric of new patterns.

Enthusiasm for regeneration and reanimation of their own culture by Indians is everywhere. The reader can experience the new Native American reality and dreams with visits to Indian country. In all parts of the state, cultures are emerging from a quiet and private existence to a more public one, with able and proud leaders; scores of inspired young dancers are led by elders who carefully teach the old ways; the results of the efforts of determined tribal and spiritual leaders in housing, health, Indian pride, and self-determination are coming into view.

We can honor their efforts by celebrating and participating in their public ceremonies and by sharing with others what is learned from the Native American cultures. The Guide will show you many places. Go and learn. 🐾

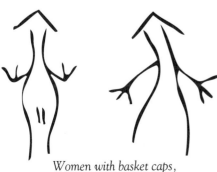

Women with basket caps,
Modoc petroglyphs - Lava Beds N.P.

▲ *The Bridge over the San Luis Rey River (Pala Reservation) remains a serviceable relic of a much earlier time.*

▲ *This wooden home on the Kashaya Rancheria (Sonoma Co.) was built in a style derived from the East Coast around 1900. Indian people at that time began to abandon traditional dwellings and began to build housing of available materials and styles.*

NATIVE CULTURE,
PERSISTENCE & TRANSITION

NATIVE CULTURES SEEN THROUGH
THEIR ARTISTIC EXPRESSION

THROUGHOUT THE STATE THE RICH VARIETY OF NATIVE CULTURES ARE EMERGING FROM LONG dormancy or quiet seclusion. Even a cursory glance can tell us that the cultures are highly varied in style and emphasis—not the same, any more than are Scot and Catalan, though both derive from tribal origens.

What is a "culture"? The term is often freely applied, as in "Celtic culture," "Navajo culture," etc., but the word deserves a deeper interpretation. In fact, most of this book is devoted to the Native American *cultures* of California. *Tribes* or *people* are not good synonyms, though many aspects of a culture are possessed by individual groups. One dictionary defines culture as: ideas, habits, and behavioral patterns, with language as the principal bond.

Following ethnographic usage, we shall use language as the major indicator of a cultural relationship. In California few of the original peoples speak their old language. English or Spanish has replaced this bonding agent; yet there are unmistakable ties among the peoples. I think we have to consider the word in two senses: the older sense (as tools, weapons, clothing, art forms, burial customs, etc.) and the broader sense as what characteristics the members of *any* group might have in common.

Let me present for your consideration some of the characteristics of a culture, those things which bind individuals into a culture, so that you may judge their pertinence to Native California cultures:
• family ties

• clan or tribal ties
• language: speakers of the old language, accents in English
• music and musical instruments
• home life: rural, urban, economic circumstance
• employment – rural, urban
• education – public, home, tribal
• art – designs in basketry, painting, wood work, architecture
• food – kind and preparation
• religion – adaptations to religions: Native, Catholic, Protestant
• beliefs:
  - shamanic use, sources of spiritual strength, tribal dance (Is it entertainment or religion?)
  - myths, superstitions, "sayings"
• person-to-person relations
  – attitude towards men, women, young, elders, outsiders (other tribes, races)
  - personality assertive or taciturn
  - sharing: "potlatch," powwows, gifts to others
  - attitude on war, games, Indian handgames, bingo

If we look and listen carefully and sensitively, we can see many of these traits and qualities of the older culture persisting in the tribal cultures of today, though always colored by the dominant culture. Through these pages, I hope to present some of the rich diversity and unity of Native California cultures.

In this section, let us explore some of the ways the Native peoples maintain traditional characteristics, their artistic expression being the ways that express their lives.

◄ *Left Page: Deer Dance Spirit, a painting by one of the best-known contemporary California Indian artists, Frank LaPena, Wintu. This painting was donated as a poster to the 1990 California Indian Conference. LaPena, as many Indian artists of today have done, derives his unique vision from aspects of traditional Indian design, religion, and spiritual values.*

▲ *Lassen Volcanic Peak, Shasta Co. (Waganupa in the Yana language)*
This outstanding gray and white landmark of ash, lava, and steam carries tales of its past
eruptions in the legends of its neighbors who hold it sacred—the Maidu, the Pit River peoples,
and the Yana.

PLACES THAT ARE DUE RESPECT
SACRED SITES, MOUNTAINS, LANDFORMS, SPECIAL PLACES, BURIAL GROUNDS

THE OLDEST PLACES, THE ONES THAT WERE TOUCHED AND WORKED BY HUMAN HANDS ages ago — so long ago that we cannot know when — demand our reverent respect. A special admiration comes to me when I realize I am witnessing the artistic work of a human being who lived a thousand or more years ago.

In California, the oldest places are nearly all rock art sites: carvings chipped into the surface (petroglyphs) or paintings (pictographs). A few known sites are of stones laid out in a pattern. All these places were selected by their artists for special purposes. Spiritual leaders tell us that the places themselves chose to be so honored — "power places." In a quiet visit to such sites, you should be able to feel the uniqueness of the place. (Go to such places with an attitude of respect and reverence, not levity or triviality.)

Most locations, especially those with numerous figures or designs, are deeply religious in nature, much as paintings, sculpture, stained glass, or symbols are used in other cultures. Imagine a shaman, priest, or religious leader, by torchlight, using symbolic petroglyphs to illustrate a point, to recall a very special event, or to teach students how to remember a certain religious rite. Imagine that certain symbols are there to be remembered at an initiation into a clan or society.

In many sites the artists used religious[5] symbols oriented to hunting — we must recall that the hunt, survival, and religion are all part of the same unbroken fabric of life. In these places we may see drawings of recognizable animals, and sometimes depictions of fanciful ones. These drawings were often used to help summon animal spirits to the place so that the hunt might be used to provide sustenance for the group.

Sites have been found in California that are astronomically related — enabling those entrusted to knowing the seasons to forecast the time, to plant, or to move camp. It was also important to know the time for certain festivals or rituals of invocation or thanksgiving.

Sometimes we find rather isolated instances of rock art: these may be simple trail directions (saying look up or down for something important), or sometimes they are a simple invocation of help to a spirit (a "shrine"). These are rock art places that we hold in respect, they are the "power places."

The burial sites of the ancestors are sacred also. Many tribes believe that spirits do not rest unless the bones remain and return to the earth whence they came. We must all respect this belief, but this respect is due all our ancestors, regardless of origin. Some tribes, such as the Maidu and the Shoshone, hasten the return, preferring to practice cremation.

In the Native American cultures or religions, some sacred places are not marked by rock art or external structure, no "edifice complex." These are the most powerful places — where one can go to receive inspiration, a "vision,"

> HAVING EXPERIENCED THE SANCTITY OF A PLACE, WE ARE IN A BETTER POSITION TO DEMAND ITS PRESERVATION.

WINTU DREAM SONG

There above, there above
At the mythical earthlodge of the south,
Spirits are wafted along the roof and fall,
Flowers bend heavily on their stems.

from ref.7, Heizer and Elsasser, p.214.

RESPECT FOR THE DEAD

Until very recent times, archaeologists dug up skeletons and bones along with the artistry the early people had created. Most modern Indian people properly objected to this desecration of the bones of their ancestors. Today, State and Federal laws have been passed that require respect for the dead; all ancient bones found in digging (of whatever origin and for whatever reason), must be reburied under the auspicies of the local Native American Heritage Commission (Sacramento). Other rock art and archaeological sites are also protected from destruction. **Heavy penalties have resulted from violation of these laws.** This author and all tribes request anyone noticing violation of these statutes to report the situation to the Commission.

[5] *These are not "magic" symbols; summoning the spirits to our attention is a religious, not a magical or miraculous act.*

▲ *The Painted Rock, in ancient Chumash land of the Carrizo Plain (Spanish, grassy), bears multicolored figures in black, red, yellow, and white. The Rock has recently been the beneficiary of a team of international petroglyph restorers. Neglected for many years, it is now under the protection of the Nature Conservancy.*

LEGENDS, MYTHS, MAGIC, AND STORIES

For the purposes of this book, I would like to offer provisional definitions for several literary and narrative terms, as I see them applied by Native Californians.

A *story* is usually a tale told to illustrate a point, attitude or allegory; or indeed it may be someone's factual account of a happening, even though it may have occurred many generations earlier. A *legend* is a story of long standing — changed, embellished, and colored by attitudes.

A *myth* is an admittedly fanciful story that deals with supernatural beings or ancestors. With some interpretation, we can extract much "truth" or even history from the mythological accounts. Doing *magic* implies exercising supernatural control over natural forces, frequently manipulating nature with evil intent.

Within the many Indian communities it is possible to hear very valuable traditional storytellers. These are persons particularly gifted at remembering the many stories, legends, and myths of their people. Fortunately, several books of their col-

lected stories are now being published for future generations, for after all, most of the storytellers are elders [6]. When you find an opportunity to listen to the stories from the elders, consider yourself very fortunate.

Among Native Americans who live in continuous and consistent contact with nature, there are special persons who have the gift of knowing deeply the properties of nature. These persons know how to use both human nature and the nature around us to improve or alter our condition, they are the "traditional" doctors of our well-being. Sometimes they are called "doctor," sometimes "shaman," sometimes "medicine person," sometimes Bill or Mary. When these persons use their talents, we are often not accustomed to their methods, so many of us acquainted with "Western medicine" are tempted to call their methods (including songs, chants, and rites) "magic." Let us resist that temptation, unless the use of sulfa drugs or nylon joint replacement is also magic.

[6] *See references 3,12,13.*

direction in one's life, or to meditate. These are natural places, where the ideas of nature embedded in the Indian culture become most evident. Frequently, they are mountaintops or summits, remote places that bring one closer to the spirits. Several mountains are well-known as "sacred" mountains (see Map I), others are held more like "reverend" mountains (Mt. Tamalpais, Mt. Boney, Mt. St. Helena, Cuyamaca Peak, Mt. Laguna). Within these places are the birds of the air, the fish of the waters, the rocks and soil and trees of the mountains — all belong to the family, everything.

The Indian people have a very difficult time preserving such places from desecration — someone always seems to want to put in a road, a beacon or radar or microwave, or a lookout. We must all learn to respect these places by going there and sensing the delight of being in a unique and sacred place. Having experienced the sanctity of a place, we are in a better position to demand its preservation, because we understand why it must be kept.

Lastly, we must respect the ancient archaeological village sites themselves, aside from the fact that they are protected by state and federal laws. A place where humans resided for hundreds or thousands of years must have some special significance. These village sites are among the ancient islands of history. If destroyed, our knowledge, realization, and imagination of what has gone before are diminished.

"To us, the ashes of our ancestors are sacred, and their resting place is hallowed ground."
—Chief Seattle (Sealth), 1855

▶ *Mt. Diablo at sunrise, seen from San Francisco. Mt. Diablo is sacred to the Miwok, Ohlone, Yokuts, and Patwin peoples—vistas from its summit encompass an area surpassed only by Mt. Kilimanjaro of East Africa. Within the State Park surrounding the peak, numerous rare and indigenous species of animal and plant life may be encountered, though hardly as plentiful today as 200 years earlier.*

▲ *Cholla cactus is an inhabitant of the desert Indian lands—it looks soft, but one touch and its tiny fishhook spines don't let go.*

THE ECOLOGICAL ENVIRONMENT

WHEN I FIRST BEGAN TO SEARCH OUT THE EXISTING INDIAN "TRUST" LAND TO write *The Earth Is Our Mother*, to my surprise I found certain large, completely uninhabited tracts, and other parcels almost undeveloped — maybe a house or two, very little more. The realization came to me that much of this land treasure had never been touched, except by the Native owners. What the California Native American communities uniquely possess, then, are in effect, large ecological preserves, a form of wilderness. Additionally, the State and National Park systems are in many places integrating into their parks an awareness of the earliest inhabitants, an awareness of Indian country.

These areas embrace deeply forested coastal zones, high mountain fastnesses, chaparral-scattered hills, unspoiled desert terrain. Not having made a careful survey of this countryside, I cannot make a detailed account of the flora and fauna contained there, but let me describe some of them.

The **Chemehuevi Reservation** occupies nearly twenty miles of Colorado River bank, and some four miles of it is devoted to an intensely-developed marina. However, if you take yourself a hundred yards up the bank, you find a desert land inhabited only by one alien species—the wild burro (which tramples the local springs, and is undesirable to the Indian game officers). The other life and countryside is almost undisturbed. Why? It is fiercely ovenlike in summer, and, to most humans, devoid of interest. But it is there, and hopefully will remain as it is, a protected desert nature reserve.

The upper reaches of the **Tule River Reservation** have been sporadically lumbered, but not clearcut. Today, timber is seldom harvested here. This area is a magnificently forested stretch of the Southern Sierra, with stark rock outcroppings towering over river valleys, and is rich in wild animals, fish, and beautiful plant life. As Indian land it will persevere in its splendor.

The **Augustine Reservation** is a square mile of the Coachella Valley desert. Some say nothing is there. Others say that this reserve of greasewood and desert scrub, occasionally hit by fires and sometimes abused by the locals, is a

---

THESE ARE PLACES WHERE THE LAND IS NOT DESPOILED, AND THE PEOPLE HAVE BEEN ABLE TO GIVE THEIR RESPECT TO THE LAND.

---

slightly blemished remnant of the early Valley; never irrigated or settled upon, it is still almost pristine. The same might be said for several sections of the nearby **Torres-Martinez Reservation.** Some sections of that reservation were submerged under the Salton Sea many years ago. Whether or not this underwater land is an ecological preserve could be the subject of debate.

Portions of the **Agua Caliente Reservation** have been quite purposefully set aside as ecological preserves — the palm canyons and their adjacent lands. These are of especially vital scientific, biological, visual, historical, and planetary interest, have been protected in the past by the tribe, and will continue to be so. All my readers, upon visiting Palm Springs, will be sure to visit these beautiful places, preserves of green nature and water in the exotic desert.

Window To The West (a private organization) is in the ancestral homeland of the Esselen people. Never under government control, the 1200-acre ranch has been kept in the family of descendants of an Esselen member of the Carmel Mission. Adjacent to the Ventana Wilderness, it is true wilderness itself, intriguing with ancient acorn grinding rocks, village sites, and painted caves. Pack trips by horseback and hikes, supervised by the tribe, explore this network of ecological preserves of immense proportions in the coastal mountains of Big Sur.

For over fifty miles upstream from the Pacific Ocean the **Yurok** and the **Hoopa Reservations** follow the Klamath and Trinity Rivers. Along this luxuriant and wild stretch of river, it is possible to see inglorious patches of clearcut forest, the land exposed like a wound. But the majority of the margins are old, if not ancient forest, especially in the vicinity of the few villages (where logging was rare). Most of the villages along these banks have been there for several *thousand* years, excepting the present houses, of course. The lands around these villages are some of California's best examples of ecological preservation in which both nature and man exist in harmony — not as "wilderness." The Indian peoples have used the riverine margins and the forests for all their subsistence needs, yet the land continues to produce appropriately, if not abused.

Other reservations have been lived in

but, once again, only lightly touched by the hand of the inhabitants, consisting only of a few homes, **Pechanga, Manzanita, Mesa Grande, Morongo, Fort Bidwell**, among many others. These are places where the natural round continues, the land is not despoiled, and the people have been able to give their respect to the land.

In some places, however, in order to provide a reasonable standard of living for its people, a tribe has found it necessary to develop the land. Such development usually takes the form of agriculture. Following successful retention of irrigation rights, large scale land-lease farming (agrobigness) has been brought to the **Fort Mojave, Colorado River Tribes, Fort Yuma**, and **Torres-Martinez Reservations** in the southland. To a much lesser extent, farming is found at **Fort Bidwell** and **Round Valley**. Though it need not be abusive, agriculture does introduce a wholly different form of ecology to the land, and it no longer can be considered an ecological preserve.

Through some recent unsavory and urgent governmental financial inducements, some tribal administrations have been under pressure to devote lands to hazardous waste dumps and other projects harmful to the earth and its beings. In its refusal to offer tribes reasonable means to a reasonable living standard, the government has thrust upon them a most degrading situation — threatened systematic degeneration and destruction of the land itself!

▲ *Top left: The many acres of leafy fields of the Ft. Yuma Reservation are possible because the Quechan people here have managed their irrigation water allotments well. Moreover, southeastern California is the warmest part of the U. S. in winter, enabling the Colorado River peoples to produce many agricultural products.*

◀ *Bottom left: The pleasant, unspoiled valley of the Tule River in spring is splashed with fog, cascades, redbuds, and wildflowers.*

▲ *California poppies cover the ruins of Soledad Mission (western Monterey Co.)*

NATIVE AMERICAN FOOD
MORE THAN FRY BREAD

ONE OF THE STRONGEST TRA-DITIONS SHARED BY ANY CULTURAL GROUP IS WHAT they eat. As you might expect, Indian food traditions in California vary widely.

In early times, before widespread oak abuse and neglect, **acorns** were a staple food, as chestnuts were in Europe. Acorns had to be dried, stored, shelled, ground, leached of tannic acid on a special bed of fern-covered leaves on sand, then cooked with hot rocks in a waterproof basket. Yes, people still do all this, and you can find acorn "mush" at most central California Indian gatherings. Personally, I think it needs some salt and herbs, but some like it straight.

Almost all California tribes used these nuts, though some types of acorns are sweeter and less tannic than others — the tan and valley oaks, in particular. We have lost many of the best trees, but the California Integrated Hardwoods Project (of which Ya-ka-ama Indian Nursery is a member) is seeking to restore a dwindling supply.

Salmon are almost a luxury to us these days, but before dams and silt-choked streams and agricultural poisons, they ran in nearly every stream in California, often twice a year. It is no wonder, then, that to the early peoples, the salmon run became a religious symbol of the renewal of the world.

> SALMON RAN IN NEARLY EVERY STREAM, OFTEN TWICE A YEAR. TO EARLY PEOPLES, THE SALMON RUN BECAME A RELIGIOUS SYMBOL OF THE RENEWAL OF THE WORLD.

Indians of northwestern California have a traditional and delicious way of baking salmon — spiking the fish on sticks, then arranging them like paddles arrayed around the fire. Once in a while the public can be treated to this specialty at festivals. Smoked salmon, or jerky, is a more common traditional fare, although genuine Indian jerky can usually be found only around Klamath, where the Yurok people produce a small amount for sale. Because of major abuse of the state's waterways, the salmon industry is fading; however, the Klamath River tribes have been struggling with the courts to preserve their traditional and legal treaty access to the source of their income and subsistence.

In central California, especially among the Pomo and their neighbors, we find another ritual food, the **strawberry**. Symbolizing the first fruits of spring, it is to this day honored in April ceremonies.

Deer hunters are about the only people familiar with **venison**, yet for some special Indian events, deep pit-roasted deer meat is provided. For such occasions, the deer has been asked by the Indians to provide food for the people, and is

▼ *The fall acorn festival at Kule Loklo offers the "treat" of acorn mush, here being prepared by local Native people.*

thanked for its "contribution," a practice which keeps us all in harmony with the earth as provider.

Further south, especially at powwows, you'll probably find **Indian tacos**. These are just like Mexican tacos, except that the bread is **fry bread**. Fry bread could best be described as a flat, puffy doughnut, rapidly deep fried to a golden brown, sometimes dribbled with honey and cinnamon.

Popular in most of the southern areas are common foods of Indian origin introduced from south of the border — the tortilla and salsa foods. On some reservations, such as Rincon, residents have planted prickly pear cactus, from whose leaves are made **nopales**, not exactly a commonly-seen food.

Lately, we have seen Indian "imports" into California, buffalo and blue corn products. Neither is a native California food, but they are here, they are of Native American origin, and they are to be enjoyed.

Some tribes bordering on the Sierra obtain (with some difficulty) **piñon nuts** from the sticky piñon pine cones of the higher and drier slopes. They are an ingredient of *pesto* sauce, but I doubt that the early peoples made that Italian specialty; instead, they roasted the nuts for a dietary staple.

▲ *(Top Right) Salmon being baked in the northern California Indian style.*

▶ *Fry bread creation at Chaw-se. Fry bread is a nearly universal Indian food in California — as the basis for a taco, or simply sprinkled with honey and spices.*

THE STRAWBERRY FESTIVAL
AT KULE LOKLO

LANNY PINOLA, THE RESIDENT KASHAYA POMO INDIAN HISTORY INTERPRETER, TELLS ME WITH A wily voice, "We've got to put up a brush enclosure around the dance arena to keep out this wind, but we're going to use real modern brush." The wind is blasting over the Point Reyes hills, up Bear Valley (Kule Loklo) at over 35 mph, and Lanny's "modern brush" consists of long plastic sheets hung on deeply-set poles. It works pretty well, but by the time the project is done, so is the blessing of the strawberries. Never mind, the Shake-head ritual to be danced later will be protected.

Indian people have gathered here from many places to dance or to participate — the occasion is Kule Loklo's Strawberry Festival, held in the "new" Coast Miwok village in Point Reyes National Seashore. They have come from Kashaya (Stewarts Point), from Colusa (in the Sacramento Valley), from El-em (Clear Lake), from local Coast Miwok and Wappo homes. Non-Indians, too, are here from many places. I hear some German and French.

Tables under the spreading laurel tree are laden with baskets of strawberries. The dancers step barefoot from their preparation ceremonies in the round-house to surround a roaring fire fanned by the wind. The eight women are wearing long white dresses with embroidery, carrying Y-shaped garlands or wearing circular ones — all woven with fresh spring flowers. They also wear colorful beaded headbands festooned with dangling ornaments, symbolic of the California quail. A man wears an unusual headdress with two very tall, blue-feather "antlers." His movements are those of a very alert deer.

The eldest of the elder ladies, Lanny's mother, bearing laurel branches and accompanied by singers, clapper sticks, and a drum, sings the song blessing the strawberries. Afterwards, she indicates that *everyone* is to partake of the extraordinarily generous offering of berries — the universal generosity of the Indian peoples.

Around the village site fine basket and bead makers are demonstrating their techniques. Cooked acorn mush is made and sampled. A different set of California Indian dancers appears and dances for an hour. These are more "secular" dances, unlike the more sacred rites earlier. The dancers will return again later, to dance long into the night.

The wind continues to roar in the tall trees. Contemplating this wind, an elder recollects that once he'd been taken to a mountaintop to let the trees teach him a song. It was very windy and sleeting. Musing for about ten minutes, he then conceded, "To hell with this, I'll come back another time," and left.

I ask one of the young dancers if she harvested strawberries. "Sorry, I've never seen any growing at home. Not even wild ones. But this is symbolic, you see, of spring and growing things and the fruits of the year provided by the Creator." And, I am thinking, of the growing goodwill spread by these people. A year later I saw strawberries growing at Kashaya.

> DANCERS STEP BAREFOOT FROM THEIR PREPARATION CEREMONIES TO CIRCLE A ROARING FIRE FANNED BY THE WIND.

◀ *The table is laden with berries awaiting the dedication songs at Kule Loklo's Strawberry Festival.*

▼ *A fine basket weaver proudly shows her intricate technique to the interested public at a Kule Loklo festival.*

HANDIWORK
BASKETS, TOOLS & BOATS

OF ALL OBJECTS THAT POSSESS HUMANNESS, THOSE THAT A PERSON HAS WORKED BY hand are the closest to the creator of the object. A basket, whatever its source, was touched, worked, formed of grasses and twigs and fibers into a piece of artistic design — sometimes only to be admired for its artistry, but usually created to serve a further purpose. California is blessed with the richest variety of basketry in the world. We have only to go to the State Indian Museum in Sacramento to see the smallest basket, made by an artist to show the world that it was possible to make a work of art bearing a design, without any "technical assistance," only 1 millimeter across. A *basket with a design!*

Baskets were made to serve all the container needs of the early peoples throughout the state who had no pottery — big conical burden baskets for hauling wood, storage baskets for seeds and grains, *watertight* baskets for water bottles and cooking, small feathered baskets for precious ornaments, beaters for seed grasses, huge granaries for acorns, baskets for hats. Not merely woven, they were filled with meaningful designs, symbols, even stories, after tribal traditions. Beyond tradition, weavers exercised artistic freedom, leaving their individual marks.

For the pure enjoyment of the senses, the ornament and jewelry makers left their marks. California's early peoples were not gold or silver workers; they worked with sinew, shells, bone, abalone, seeds, feathers, and a few pretty stones. The works of art they produced have a quiet glow, not glitz. Well, some of the modern ones have glitz, as you will discover at the craft booths.

Care went into forming tools from wood and stone — handles, levers, arrows, bows, and beautifully-chipped projectile points. The artistic content here consists mostly of the beauty of the form itself, although a few tools were lavishly decorated.

Boats were objects worthy of particular artistic attention. The traditional art of carving a canoe for a northwestern river is nearly lost, but has been preserved by a few Yurok boatmakers. A rare opportunity to watch the creation of a redwood canoe occasionally presents itself at a reservation or national park festival. It is an event not to be missed.

A form of basketry went into boatmaking in lakes and estuaries of central California — the tule reed boat. Used for transportation or fishing, they were nearly identical to those of the Quechua and Aymara of Lake Titicaca in South America, a reed raft with turned-up bow and stern. A few modern reconstructions of Ohlone and Pomo design exist in museums. All have been found to be water-worthy.

Chumash shipbuilding artists constructed 30-foot oceangoing *tomols* to carry passengers and steatite to and from their offshore islands. These boats were unabashedly decorated with abalone, glued on with asphalt (from the Santa Barbara oozes) or pitch from pine sap. You can see examples in Santa Barbara in the Natural History Museum and in the Courthouse.

> NOT MERELY WOVEN, BASKETS INCLUDED MEANINGFUL DESIGNS, SYMBOLS, EVEN STORIES.

▲ *Judy Ramos, the former curator of the striking Pomo Culture Center at Lake Mendocino, near Ukiah. This Center is a good first stopping.*

▲ *Southwesterly in downtown San Francisco is a good example of Indian craft shops that deal exclusively with Native American artists.*

ARTISANS, STORYTELLERS, MURALISTS & MODERN ARTISTS

It is one thing to look at the finished product, but far more stimulating and exciting to *see* the artist create. A closer relationship to the culture itself arises from watching a basket take shape, a dance performed, or from listening to a story firsthand by the fire light of a gathering. At most Indian gatherings you can experience such things, and Indian artists will usually proudly share their artistic creation. Consult the Events Calendar for opportunities.

In the arts of painting and sculpture we more likely see the finished product of the artist's work: murals, paintings, drawings, poster art, lithographs, sculptures, and woodworking. Dozens of Native artists reside in California, and exhibit and sell their work. Galleries that show Native American work are rare, but read on.

San Francisco and Los Angeles are centers for muralists, and their work commonly contains political and/or cultural references. The cultural references are largely to the Native American communities of North, Central, and South America. Their rich mural tradition comes to us largely from Mexico and Central America — more specifically, from the ancient Maya and Aztec, through the masters Diego Rivera, David Alfaro Siqueiros, José Clemente Orozco, and others of the school of Mexico City. Muralists can be located through local Native American or Hispanic Cultural Centers in the cities, or the Yellow Pages.

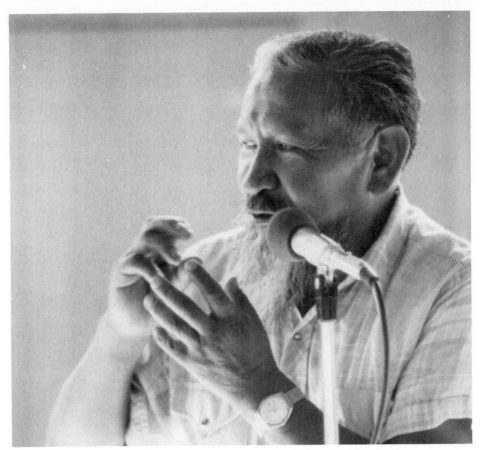

▲ *A storyteller can stir the imagination as well as relate the legends and tales that are a large part of a tribe's heritage.*

▲ *Bernice Torres, a Pomo spiritual leader, sings Kashaya Pomo songs for her listeners at the San Juan Bautista Indian Market.*

▲ It is a particularly pleasing experience to purchase artwork from an artist, especially when the work is created in front of you—here at the San Juan Bautista Indian Market.

Tribal origins of the artists:
Top Left: Jemez Pueblo (New Mexico), Mickey Vallo
Top Right: Makah (Washington),Ben Della
Bottom Left: Acoma Pueblo (New Mexico), potter Alida Pérez
Bottom Right: Quiche Maya (Guatemala), Yolanda Hernandez

THE SAN JUAN BAUTISTA
ALL-INDIAN MARKET

SOUTH FROM GILROY, THE FUZZY FOOTHILLS OF THE COAST RANGE ARE BACKED BY HIGH RIDGES that will block the straight lines of Highway 101. Here I loop off the freeway and head southeastward through the flat pepper and tomato fields, driving on top of the San Andreas fault. My destination is in sight: perched on a little shelf above the greening fields is the little red-tile-roofed mission town of San Juan Bautista, founded by Padre Fermin Lasuén in 1797. The site is the ancient Mutsun Ohlone village of Xumontwash, but nobody in San Juan seems to know that.

I drive into the parking lot/campground, partly enclosed by an adobe wall which is slowly dissolving over time; the skies above are threatening to accelerate the dissolution with a deluge. None comes. In other years, the market was held in April, and storms sent everyone scurrying inside cramped quarters. Elaine and Sonne Reyna (Comanche), the market's directors, struggling mightily to present this market for many years, moved the date later, hoping the skies would cooperate. With hope and prayers to the Great Spirit, they do.

The annual Indian spring market does not disappoint my expectations — rows upon rows of beautiful artistry set under the olive-laden trees of the 200-year-old mission. The speckled shade enhances the artwork in the sixty-five stalls — sparkling and brilliant — the crafting and artistry of hundreds of Indian talents.

To savor the place I walk around, just quickly, looking to see what to my wondering eyes should appeal. Silver and turquoise — massive, or tiny and delicate. Black and lustrous Hopi silver.

> **ROWS UPON ROWS OF BEAUTIFUL ARTISTRY ARE SET OUT UNDER THE OLIVE-LADEN TREES OF THE MISSION. INDIAN DRUMS BOOM — FOR THE FIRST TIME IN 200 YEARS.**

Glacier-blue lapis. Rare polished clamshell necklaces. Fancy beadwork. Guatemalan and Peruvian Indian embroidery and patterned fabrics — new and old and made into clothing, rugs, purses. Bold and soft posters of Indian life. Tile work. Pueblo pottery. Basket weavers weaving beautiful baskets in non-traditional dark colors or in traditional California style. New ideas — amber and bamboo jewelry from Mexico, bright orange and blue mother-of-pearl in angular designs. Lakota ceremonial and battle axes. Books on Indian lore, crafts, history. On the recommendation of a Southwestern Indian co-op merchant, I buy one on rock art interpretation, a neglected field. A feast for the eyes.

Then for the rest of your body: B-B-Q chicken with all the trimmings, Indian tacos, fry bread, buffalo burgers. The drifting smells of food, incense, and sage enhance the art.

The booming of drums comes from near the church cloisters. Xipe Totec, the Aztec dancers, in plumed and gilded costume are dancing their energetic, rhythmic dances, seemingly tireless. They dance because they must, they say. The dancers appear several times during the two-day market; some of the vendors grumble that they lose the buying crowd, while they go to watch. Another drum sounds — this time Lakota songs on the big bass drum — from a quartet who drove all the way from South Dakota. Feasts for the eyes *and* ears.

Later, while I rest in the pretty mission flower gardens, the Spanish priest happens by. "We like to let the Indians use the ground for free. It's good for both them and the church." On the other side of the church there is a simple wooden plaque: "Buried in this sacred ground in unmarked graves are 4,300 Mission Indians..."

I wander into the simply-furnished old mission before Mass time; the Indian drums boom just outside — for the first time in 200 years.

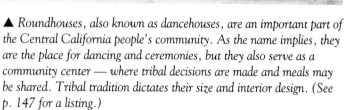

▲ *Roundhouses, also known as dancehouses, are an important part of the Central California people's community. As the name implies, they are the place for dancing and ceremonies, but they also serve as a community center — where tribal decisions are made and meals may be shared. Tribal tradition dictates their size and interior design. (See p. 147 for a listing.)*

Top Left: *An unusual sod-covered Coast Miwok roundhouse at Kule Loklo.*

Top Right: *Oak smoke, pine needles, the ray of light from the smokehole penetrating the shadows—the return to Mother Earth.*

Bottom Left: *Maidu Roundhouse. The roundhouse is the Indian community center and a comfortable place to play.*

Bottom Right: *Spring rains add color to the roundhouse dances in the Sacramento River Valley.*

A SPRING GATHERING
IN THE CENTRAL VALLEY

THE FIRST WEEK IN MAY I AM INVITED TO JOIN A SMALL GATHERING OF INDIAN PEOPLE IN A Sacramento Valley Indian village. It is time to dance, and to give the roundhouse its first big "dedication," even though it has been up for a while and has already been used for some dancing. Dance time means that banners are to be flying from the flagpole. Stars and crosses and crescents fly in the wind.

Unfortunately, the wind also brought a late spring deluge, which revealed some incompleteness in the roofing. The entranceway had become a quagmire. I arrive just after a round of dancing, which ended about the time a downpour poured. Kids are out front in their bare feet, having a ball squishing and splashing the new mud out of the entrance, shoveling up the gunk, and tossing it into the yard. A truckload of gravel is mysteriously found and applied to the walkway. Fine.

About this time, the dinner break is announced. Tables are brought into the roundhouse and loaded with turkey, venison, meatballs in sauce, rice pilaf, mashed potatoes, broccoli sauteed in meat bits, a huge pot of acorn soup, tubs of coffee, berry and fruit pies, fry bread... Delicious cuisine prepared by the host family is offered to all guests, the universal generosity of the Indian peoples.

Now it's time to dance again. The floor is swept; the fire is stoked with fresh oak branches, the smoke forming a huge undulating cloud, like an inverted lake, at the top of the roundhouse. Outside, the clouds retreat; a late sunbeam flashes a double rainbow over the gathering. Inside, odors blend from the oak smoke and the fresh tule canes from the nearby riverbank.

Ee-e-e. We — huh! The dancers and singers are ready. Three Big Head cycles are followed by a Flat Head. The Big Heads are terribly imposing — a spray of white feathers mounted on the tips of willow branches — like a dancing dogwood tree in full bloom. The "leader," Big Head's companion, carries a bow in one hand and a quiver of arrows wrapped in a fox skin in the other. Both dancers move as deer or birds — short, sharp, alert motions, tied to one another by an invisible thread. Tonight, the rapid, insistent pounding of the huge drum (a hollow wooden box set above a small rectangular trench in the floor) and the intense singing of the accompaniment are augmented by the sizzling patter of rain. Raindrops spit at the fire, dampening nothing. Singers and dancers, old and young alike, toss coins into the arena and stand to dance at the edges of the dance arena. The youngsters, all very intense, are perfectly behaved.

Midnight break. Sandwiches, spaghetti, corn on the cob, cake, colas, coffee. Then, a short, warm healing ceremony given in the old language. At about 1:30 A.M., a "double head" — two Big Head dancers perform, or rather, become the dance spirit, somehow meshing and separating, dancing around the fire. Their clapper sticks are furious. A comment from the back: "Them rattlesnakes sure are angry." Chuckles from the people. I suddenly realize that they really do radiate the sound of rattlesnakes, a creature highly respected by the Central California peoples.

Next morning after breakfast in the roundhouse, the storms pass over, the kids play kickball on the grass, grown cats nuzzle the dogs warming themselves in the sun. I've not heard a discouraging word both days, and I know I'm in the Peaceable Kingdom.

▲ *The Big Head dance is one of the most mystical dances of all the California Indian ceremonies.*

▲ *Dancers at Chaw-se California Indian Days.*

MUSICIANS & DANCERS

THE MUSICAL INSTRUMENTS OF THE EARLY PEOPLES WERE MOSTLY PERCUSSION, ALONG WITH TWO winds, and one string. They are easily made, evoking natural sounds, and are usually played in association with ceremonial rites.

Every tribe and group used flutes — some wooden, some cane or elderberry stem, some of bone. These were the melody makers, but they are very seldom heard these days. When they are, we hear plaintive and nostalgic songs, often mixed with influences of later times. The simplest of flutes, the whistle (often doubled), is still played at many ceremonies over all parts of California. The whistle is sometimes the sound of wind, sometimes of birds. A rare "D" shaped, twanged, one-string bow sometimes accompanied individuals in meditation, the open mouth a resonator, but this is not heard at all any more.

The most commonly seen instrument is the split-stick clapper, made from a hollow resonant elderberry or cane stalk. The stalk is slit lengthwise, with an opening for a more resounding *clack!* This is the basic rhythm section; the slap of the stick is the small drum. Vibrated softly, the clapper is an attention-getter. But vibrated vigorously, the clapper becomes the rattlesnake, and is the Native way of paying respect to the animal that moves with ease between the earth and the underworld, and is respected by all other animals.

In the roundhouse, the big drum is formed from a trench in the floor covered (today) by a sheet of plywood and struck by a large pole with a tip of burlap or leather. This drum is placed off-center, where the sound best reverberates within the room. In the symbolism of all things in the Native world, this drum is the sound of the bear, to whom respect is paid by drumming.

Smaller skin-covered drums we see at almost all Indian ceremonies and at handgames are considered "imports" from east of California, although they arrived here a hundred years ago. Their use has become nearly universal these days, since their resonance and tone quality are more musical than most of the more traditional rhythm-makers. The huge "bass" drums that are laid on their sides are recent imports from the Plains Indian tribes.

You can certainly tell the difference from California music in the songs that are sung with them as well. The drums we see played most energetically in California today are those of the Nahuatl-speaking Aztec dancers. This tall, tight-skinned drum and the syncopated rhythmic style came from Mexico quite recently. Many, many Native Americans from south of the border are familiar with the persuasion these drums radiate.

Individual dancers enhance their movements with rattles made of many resonant materials — gourds and turtle shells and pottery (from the south); deer and goat toenails; moth cocoons; and seed pods. Groups of smaller objects like deer hooves are bound together to give larger, louder sounds.

There is one truly *wind* instrument, the bull-roarer. This is a wooden blade, attached to a long cord or thong, and twirled round and round, producing a zzzzz like a cicada, like a mammoth bumble-bee, like impending thunder. Some shamans use this instrumental

▲ *The Big Head dance, seen here at an unusual outdoor setting.*

▲ *Dancers in the roundhouse at Chaw-se.*

▲ *A bare foot connects the dancer to Mother Earth.*

sound for a danger signal, others for summoning the people to events. Kids use it, too.

Earlier, I mentioned that few instruments are played solo; instead, they accompany singing and/or dancing. The singing of songs in the ancient languages is not a lost art, and I think it is an art being regained. With some tribes, much has been lost over the past century, but everywhere I look, I see major efforts to teach the old songs and traditions to the children and younger tribal members. Songs, the right songs, accompany the Jumping Dances, the Brush Dances, the Big Head, the Flathead, the Kuksu, the Hesi, the Cahuilla and Quechan Birdsongs. The songs are remembered by the elders; the younger people learn and continue them.

Where there is a will to survive, there you will find music. Where you find music, there is dance as well. Dance is the ultimate expression bonding Native Americans to their tradition and culture. Dance is so strong a tie that leaders of non-Native religions have tended to wish ill upon the dance, even to the point of extinguishing it. The dancers, however, continue. They are our threads from past to future.

Indian musicians, not surprisingly, also play modern music. Probably because of their rural background, a number of Natives have become country/western musicians — I've found all-Indian bands in Bishop and Winterhaven, and quite a few individuals are members of bands. It was surprising to find several accomplished guys playing jazz and blues. Listening to their riffs, the blues come naturally. Rock bands are out there, too, but pinning them down is like pointing to flying birds.

▲ *Lady dancers at Chaw-se show their traditional dress*

▲ *Shawl dancers await their turn at an evening powwow at the August Sierra Mono Indian Fair.*

BINGO!

ABOUT 1 A.M. ONE COOL NIGHT IN MOMBASA, KENYA, I WAS AWAKENED BY LOUD SOUNDS coming from a loudspeaker on the sidewalk below my hotel window, peculiar sporadic bursts of words and numbers in Swahili. Dragging myself to the window, I was astonished to be witnessing a local men's club's midnight bingo game. But that was not like this night near Palm Springs.

A hush descends over the huge room, so well lit that no shadows are permitted. You hold your little 5 by 5 card marked with numbered squares and finger a felt pen with a huge mushy tip. From a little cage at the far wall the letters and numbers bellow out: B-8 (mush), G-46 (no mush), N-31 (no mush)... Someone yells BINGO! From her corner of the long table spontaneous screams rise to wake the dead. The cardholder has tempted fate and won the Megabingo jackpot — $500,000.

Oh well, I think, next one; and pull out yet another card from the pack.

This scenario could happen just about any night at any of the six California Indian Megabingo halls that are tied by satellite to the nationwide Indian bingo network. "Mega at 10:35 EST nightly" read the flyers. For stakes up to $10,000 or more, or less, you can try most of the fourteen other California "regular" Indian bingo halls.

There have been many modern attempts to pull the Indian out of the economic canyon, some constructive, others destructive — employment crusades, timber and mining schemes, small business development. Few of these seemed to work to the betterment of the tribe members. Until along came bingo — for the fortunate few.

High-stakes bingo originated with the daring of a group of Florida Seminoles in 1981. Here was a way to cater to the gaming instinct of a lot of people in a big way. Along came the hurdles, also. The game had to be high stakes, but most states wouldn't allow that. But then, Indian reservations aren't state land, nor exactly federal land, either. They are Indian land.

To get an audience, there has to be a nearby population base without access to big gambling. We're not talking Vegas or state lotteries or some remote rez; we're talking Miami, L.A., Tulsa, or Minneapolis. The stakes have to be high enough to pull people out of the city, as big as most lotteries, and there has to be *live* action. Who's going to set it all up? Most enterprises capable of setting up such operations don't have noses clean enough for the Federal bureaus who will have ultimate oversight.

In 1983, two years after the Florida venture had successfully gained its legal footing, high-stakes Indian gaming (as poker) was introduced into California by an "immigrant" from the Florida venture, Mark Nichols, and his father John, an economist. A card parlor was opened at the Cabazon Reservation in Indio, sparking round after round of legal challenges to state and federal law, and to Indian sovereignty. An appeal of the

> SOMEONE YELLS BINGO! FROM HER CORNER OF THE LONG TABLE, SPONTANEOUS SCREAMS RISE TO WAKE THE DEAD.

case on Indian sovereignty versus state and local laws went all the way to the Supreme Court, who in February 1987, found in favor of the tribe. Not only was their card parlor legal, so was high-stakes bingo.

Once the legal grounds were laid, California Indian reservations from Trinidad to Fort Yuma recognized the opportunity to raise a comfortable income for their members. Even though Indian gambling establishments undoubtedly provide income, they are not without detractions. Not long ago, a Congressionally-directed investigation of several operations forced closure of four, at least temporarily. Fraud, described as "wrongly-paid contracts," seemed to have been the main concern.

A s one reservation project director told me, So much money in one place is *bound* to cause things to go bad; he, for one, would rather not see *any* bingo on his reservation. The trouble is with operations: although the director must be a local tribesperson, the operating skills, personnel management, security, and accounting are usually handled by an outside organization, with a payroll of from 25 to 350 persons. Some of these outside organizations have alleged ties to people with less than impeccable credentials.

Another approach, taken by some, is to operate virtually all tasks by tribal members. Prudent measures like this and careful supervision over all operations have kept most bingo halls clean.

A typical bingo hall is a comfortable,

neat, gymnasium-sized space with rows of long tables. The all-important announcer's platform forms the center of one wall. Anywhere from 1,000 to 2,500 guests are present; larger halls provide a snack bar or a dining room offering American food at very reasonable prices. Halls operate from three to seven days a week, and their parking lots seem to have several tour buses of players drawn from the nearest urbs.

What does the operation generate for the members of the tribe? For a small tribe, some members can receive a monthly per capita distribution of $5,000, but that varies.

How do Indians feel about the high-stakes bingo on their reservation? If there is any one activity common to the Indians of California, or of the U.S., for that matter, it is gambling. But their traditional kind of gambling is radically different from the high-tech, big business of bingo. Indian hand games or guessing games call for a deeply psychic milieu and require intense concentration, not just listening to numbers with felt tip in hand. (See p. 74.) Not many Indians regularly play bingo; they would rather enjoy the fruits of the enterprise. Nichols notes that he recognizes about 30% of his players on any one night, and maybe 85% are returnees. In response to my query if these are addicts, he pointed out that most are using bingo for pleasant socializing, and enjoy a good adrenalin rush.

How many cards would you like tonight? $12 for 25 cards, $3 for 3... 🐎

HOW MANY CARDS WOULD YOU LIKE TONIGHT? $12 FOR 25 CARDS, $3 FOR 3.

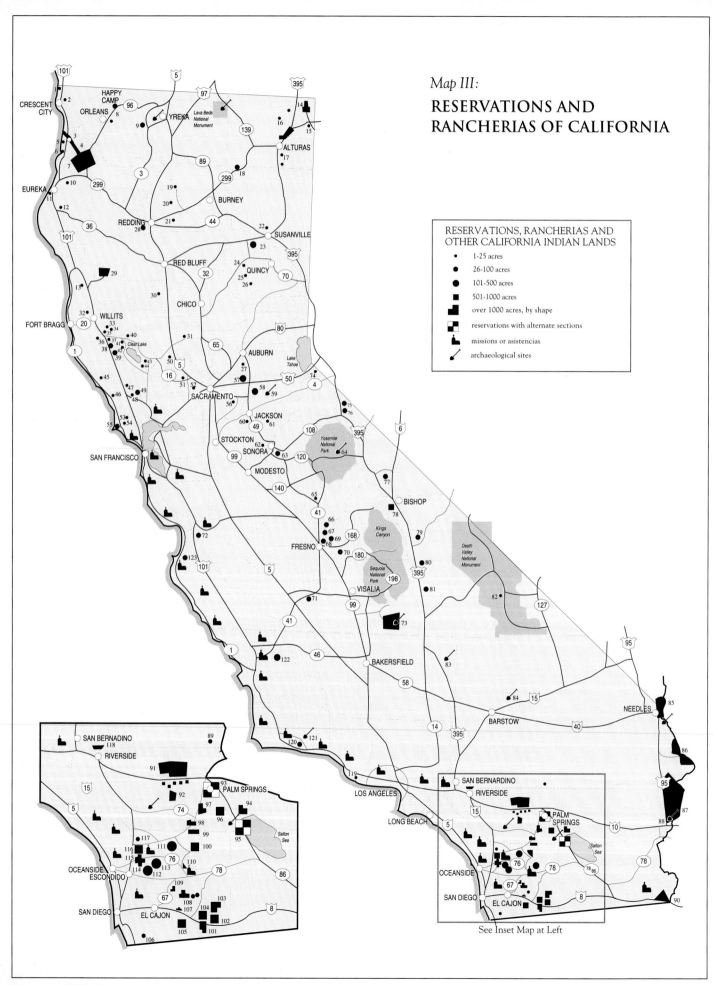

Map III:

RESERVATIONS AND RANCHERIAS OF CALIFORNIA

RESERVATIONS, RANCHERIAS AND
OTHER CALIFORNIA INDIAN LANDS

- 1-25 acres
- 26-100 acres
- 101-500 acres
- 501-1000 acres
- over 1000 acres, by shape
- reservations with alternate sections
- missions or asistencias
- archaeological sites

See Inset Map at Left

RESERVATION AND RANCHERIAS OF CALIFORNIA

NORTHWEST

1 Smith River Rancheria
2 Elk Valley (Crescent City Rancheria)
3 Resighini Rancheria
4 Yurok Reservation
5 Big Lagoon Rancheria & Sumeg Village
6 Tsurai (Trinidad) Rancheria
7 Hoopa Valley Reservation
8 Karuk Tribe (Orleans, Happy Camp, 6 other parcels)
9 Quartz Valley Rancheria
10 Blue Lake Rancheria
11 Table Bluff Rancheria
12 Rohnerville Rancheria
13 Laytonville Rancheria

NORTHEAST

14 Ft. Bidwell Reservation
15 Cedarville Rancheria
Pit River Tribes:
16 XL Ranch Rancheria
17 Alturas & Likely Rancherias
18 Lookout Rancheria
19 Big Bend Rancheria
20 Roaring Creek Rancheria
21 Montgomery Creek Rancheria

22 Susanville Rancheria
23 Greenville Rancheria
24 Berry Creek Rancheria
25 Enterprise Rancheria
26 Mooretown Rancheria

CENTRAL COAST & CENTRAL VALLEY

North of I-80
28 Redding Rancheria
29 Round Valley Reservation
30 Grindstone Creek Rancheria
31 Colusa Rancheria
32 Sherwood Valley Rancheria
33 Potter Valley Rancheria
34 Redwood Valley Rancheria
35 Coyote Valley Rancheria
36 Pinoleville Rancheria
37 Guidiville Rancheria
38 Yo-ka-yo Rancheria
39 Hopland Rancheria
40 Scotts Valley Rancheria
41 Upper Lake Rancheria
42 Robinson Rancheria

43 Big Valley Rancheria
44 El-em (Sulphur Bank) Indian Colony
45 Manchester and Point Arena Rancherias
46 Kashaya (Stewarts Point) Rancheria
47 Cloverdale Rancheria
48 Dry Creek Rancheria
49 Middletown Rancheria
50 Cortina Rancheria
51 Rumsey Rancheria
52 D-Q University
53 Ya-ka-ama (Education Center)
54 Graton Rancheria
27 Auburn Rancheria

South of I-80
55 Kule Loklo (Point Reyes National Seashore)
56 Wilton Rancheria
57 Shingle Springs Rancheria
58 Jackson Rancheria
59 Chaw-Se (Grinding Rocks State Park)
60 Buena Vista Rancheria
61 Sheepranch Rancheria
62 Chicken Ranch Rancheria
63 Tuolumne Rancheria
64 Ahwahnee Village (Yosemite National Park)
65 Wassama Roundhouse (State Park)
66 N. Fork Rancheria & Sierra Mono Museum
67 Picayune Rancheria
68 Big Sandy (Auberry) Rancheria
69 Table Mountain Rancheria
70 Cold Springs Rancheria
71 Santa Rosa Rancheria
72 Indian Canyon
73 Tule River Reservation

EAST OF THE SIERRA DIVIDE

74 Alpine Washoe Reservation
75 Camp Antelope Community
76 Bridgeport Indian Colony
77 Benton Paiute Reservation
78 Bishop Reservation
79 Big Pine Reservation
80 Ft. Independence Reservation
81 Lone Pine Reservation
82 Timbi-sha Shoshone Band (Death Valley National Park)
83 Coso Hot Springs Pictograph Site
84 Calico Early Man Site

MOJAVE DESERT, COACHELLA VALLEY, AND THE COLORADO RIVER

85 Ft. Mojave Reservation
86 Chemehuevi Reservation
87 Colorado River Tribes
88 Desert Intaglios Site
89 Twentynine Palms Reservation
90 Ft. Yuma Reservation
91 Morongo Reservation
92 Soboba Reservation
93 Agua Caliente Reservation
94 Cabazon Reservation
95 Torres-Martinez Reservation & Fish Traps
96 Augustine Reservation
97 Santa Rosa Reservation
98 Ramona Reservation
99 Cahuilla Reservation

SOUTHWESTERN CALIFORNIA AND THE SOUTHERN COAST

100 Los Coyotes Reservation
101 Campo Reservation
102 Manzanita Reservation
103 La Posta Reservation
104 Cuyapaipe
105 Sycuan Resvation
106 Jamul Indian Village
107 Viejas Reservation
108 Capitan Grande, Inaja, & Cosmit Reservations
109 Barona Reservation
110 Santa Ysabel Reservation
111 Mesa Grande Reservation
112 San Pascual Reservation
113 Rincon Reservation
114 La Jolla Reservation
115 Pala & Mission Reserve Reservations
116 Pauma & Yuima Reservations
117 Pechanga Reservation
118 San Manuel Reservation
119 Satwiwa (Santa Monica Mountains National Recreation Area)
120 Santa Ynez Reservation
121 Chumash Painted Cave
122 Red Wind
123 Pa-ché-pus (Esselen Ranch)

A GLOSSARY OF TERMS

GROUPING PEOPLE BY THEIR ANCESTRAL LANGUAGE HAS BECOME A UNIVERSAL CUSTOM tom among linguists, anthropologists and ethnologists, and I will follow that usage in this book. Map I shows the linguistic relationships of the early inhabitants of the state, to the best knowledge of researchers. A few groups similar in other cultural respects spoke different languages, and some similar dialects were spoken by rather different peoples, but early language remains the best basis for cultural correlation.

Most Native groups in California were not organized into large tribal entities, such as Lakota, Hopi, or Cherokee; rather, the people here existed in smaller, self-governing groups, in territories usually determined by geography and ecology. Consequently, we do not use the word *tribe* in the same sense as it is applied east and north of California. For larger language groupings we use *peoples*, as in the Pomo or Cahuilla peoples. *Tribe* is reserved for the residents of a particular community, as in the Coyote Valley Pomo Tribe or the Santa Rosa Cahuilla Tribe. There are exceptions to these usages, as in the Mohave Tribe (the Hamákhava or Mohave people who live nearly entirely on their large reservation).

People: Groups which speak (or spoke) a specific language or similar dialects. East of California this grouping is called a *tribe*.

Tribe, Band, Colony, Community: The group of persons residing in a particular reservation, rancheria, or community. *Not* the usage east of California, such as Sioux (Lakota), or Navajo (Diné).

Chairperson or Spokesperson (chief or chieftain is no longer used): The presiding member of a tribal council (including some tribes without land).

Ranchería: A small reservation, usually large enough only for residences and tiny garden plots. (Originally, Spanish for an Indian village.)

Trust land: Indian land held by the Federal Government (BIA) in "trust" for the people.

Allotted land: Land lying within the boundaries of a reservation which is under direct control of individuals, "owned" by an Indian person or persons, as opposed to communal ownership.

Terminated land: Former trust land that has passed into private, usually non-Indian ownership. When Indian land is terminated and deeds are issued to the resident Indians, they generally lose certain rights normally afforded reservation residents, such as housing assistance, education, tax exemption, health services, utility connections, and certain kinds of welfare and unemployment benefits. In 1984, numerous formerly "terminated" lands were returned to trust status, owing to government mishandling of the termination process.

A GUIDE TO CALIFORNIA INDIAN COUNTRY

THE NATIVE AMERICAN PEOPLES UNDERSTAND A CONTINUOUS THREAD OF EXISTENCE BETTER than most cultures. Most tribal groups in California have not been displaced far from their ancestral homes. Remnants of earlier times are all around; the historical context stretches further and is more easily traced than that of many European, Asian, and African peoples. Here, today, we have the opportunity to see the world of the descendants of the original Californians.

In many ways, it is a world of beauty, order, and tradition, even though that tradition has suffered immense assaults, changes, and adaptations. That thread of continuity of ancestors, of spirit, of time, of place, and of the harmony of all things persists; life is continuous and whole, as is tradition, and cannot be compartmentalized. Although "science" is fond of dividing things for study, as: archaeology-anthropology-ethnology, mind-spirit-body, or animal-vegetable-mineral, Native traditions cannot be meaningfully subjected to this type of scrutiny.

In this book and this guide, I will attempt to present contemporary California Indian Country in all its time dimensions. What you can see here and now can be representative or evocative of what has been, what is, and possibly, what may become. You can see where the earliest Indians fished or made arrows, where ancient peoples painted their symbols onto rock, where later peoples built their villages and homes. You can be near the sacred spaces in the mountains, rocks, and springs where the sacred meets the profane. You can see where people live today, what they do that may or may not be like what you know or expect.

> MOST TRIBAL GROUPS HAVE NOT BEEN DISPLACED FAR FROM THEIR ANCESTRAL HOMES. THE THREAD OF CONTINUITY PERSISTS.

You can find sublime beauty or simple drabness in the settings of the present-day Indian communities. But in all of them, you can find the direct descendants of a people who have kept their identity. Throughout California, you can find the old spirits reawakened; the people will dance and pray and hold their ceremonies — because they must.

Language designations shown for residents of reservations and rancherias are those assigned at the time of their federal recognition. Since then, intermarriage and migration have altered the original character of nearly all locations. It is with great satisfaction that we can still find native speakers in many places.

NORTHWESTERN
CALIFORNIA

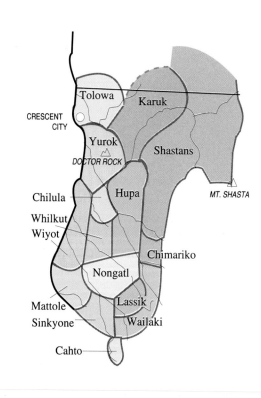

LANGUAGE KEY

Hokan

Athapascan

Ritwan

Tolowa

Karuk

CRESCENT
CITY

Yurok

DOCTOR ROCK

Shastans

Chilula

Hupa

MT. SHASTA

Whilkut

Wiyot

Chimariko

Nongatl

Mattole

Lassik

Sinkyone

Wailaki

Cahto

THE PEOPLES

THE RESERVATIONS & ORGANIZATIONS

Athapaskan Speakers [a]

Tolowa

Smith River* and Elk Valley*
Rancherias;
organization: Tolowa Nation

Hupa/Chilula/Whilkut

Hoopa Reservation;
organization: South Fork Hupa

Wailaki

Round Valley Reservation*

Mattole/Nongatl/Lassik/Sinkyone
(The "Eel River Tribes")

Rohnerville Rancheria*,
though largely without trust lands

Cahto

Laytonville Rancheria

Hokan Speakers [b]

Shasta

Quartz Valley Rancheria*,
though largely without trust lands
organization: Shasta Nation

Karuk

Orleans Res. and Happy Camp Tribal
Center, plus 6 other parcels

Chimariko

(none)

Algic Languages [c]

Wiyot

Table Bluff, Rohnerville*, and Blue Lake*
Rancherias

Yurok

Yurok Reservation, Resighini,
Big Lagoon, Tsurai, Smith River*,
Elk Valley*, Blue Lake* Rancherias

* Shared with other groups

[a] Athapaskan is a language group related to such diverse peoples as Tlingit (Alaska), Diné (Navajo), and Apache.

[b] Hokan is an ancient language group found in diverse areas of the state, and is distantly related to groups of northern and central Mexico.

[c] Algic Languages are related to Ritwan-Algonkian and are distantly related to languages of the central and eastern U.S.

THE PEOPLES OF NORTHWESTERN CALIFORNIA

"THE NORTH COAST IS A COLD COAST, AND A WILD ONE," SAID A POET OF THE English shores. The description applies here, too. Further up the conifer-blanketed slopes and great river valleys, so often layered-over with a soft gray ceiling of fog, the forest is more mottled by the deciduous trees of the warmer uplands, then the land opens to wide oak savannahs. This variety of ecologies is the northwest—abundant with salmon and eel, shellfish, shorebirds, deer and elk, reeds and rushes, redwoods and fir and oak — all the riches of nature's stores only a short walk from home. This is the land in which the ancestors settled thousands of years ago. These are the lands where hundreds of Indian peoples of California still live today.

Life in the villages was varied, as was the topography. The Tolowa people built huge seagoing canoes for fishing and trading. The Yurok had a tradition of great river canoe building. The people of the lower river and seacoast villages built sturdy wooden homes, partly sunken for protection from weather and bears (see p. 26), and were manifestly earth-oriented.

Most villages built and used sweathouses, also partly sunken, and smaller than a house. These were not saunas, but places that served as village

▶ *The mouth of the Klamath River is ancient Yurok country. The old fishing village of Requa lies below us; the marshes along the shores abound with deer, birds, and grasses, and the tidewater flats have always been excellent fishing grounds. Above us is the Klamath River entrance to Redwood National Park.*

community centers: for inspiration, tribal decision-making, meditation, relaxation, health, and a place for handiwork. They were generally male-dominated, but sometimes opened to women for special or important occasions. After all, most of the doctors in the northwest were women, or men (*wergern*) who had "crossed over" and adopted women's ways to become healers. The wergern, also known as *berdache*, are given special recognition, since they possess both male and female qualities. It is said that some shamans (doctors-priests-pharmacists) in the neighborhood were able to work either evil or good, and were held to account for their deeds.

A more communally-used place was the dancehouse — a powerful symbol of the earth-oriented cultures. These were (and are) larger structures (see p. 26), and not every village had one. In the center is placed the fire-pit, opening to the center of the earth. In this tectonic land where seismic and volcanic activity are frequent and destructive, and in a land from which all sustenance is derived, the earth-center is an important place to honor. The dancehouse was the "cultural" center where religious and more secular dances were held. (See p. 62 on the dance.) Other dances were held in the open, in a covered pit arena with sloping sides, like a very small foot-

THE GRASS OR HAND GAME

Two teams sit facing each other equipped with the following: two pairs of two "bones," one of each marked with a ring; a set of ten or twelve playing sticks; an object to drum upon (either a small hand drum or, more traditionally, a log and sticks). At one time, the bones were hidden with a hand-held sheaf of grass, but today the players use a shawl. The objective is to obtain all the playing sticks and the bones by guessing which hand holds the marked bone. Meanwhile, an elaborate process of passing the sticks back and forth occurs.

Before the game begins, bets are placed by supporters and members of each side. (All bets must be covered by an equal amount on the other side, and are recorded). The winning side takes all: double or nothing. The bets are tied in a bundle and tossed to one end of the "playing field."

One side chooses a "guesser," always someone known to have great powers of accuracy in guessing, since a lot of money may be riding on the outcome.

On the other side, two persons are chosen to conceal the bones; it is hoped they will have sufficient negative thought powers to deflect the other team's guesser. (In my experience, a good guesser can always "see" through anyone who is neither serious nor sober.)

The side holding the bones begins drum-ming and chanting. The songs are almost always in the ancient languages, and are frequently amusing or sarcastic: "You couldn't guess your way — out of an open tent." The music should set up a psychic shield, deflecting the mind of the guesser from the "truth" of the bones. The guesser takes plenty of time to be sure, and then...

The moment of truth: the guesser subtly indicates by direction of the thumb or a playing stick what is believed to be the positions of the two marked bones in the hands of the two hiders, there being four possible outcomes (right-right, left-left, right-left outside, and left-right inside). Watch carefully, for a sly holder can sometimes fool the guessing team. Whoever "wins," gets either bones or sticks. If the guesser fails, his side surrenders sticks; if he succeeds, bones or sticks are surrendered to his team. Ultimately all the sticks must be obtained.

With two teams of nearly equal power, a game can go on for an hour or more, and the sticks change sides many times. (One tactic is to partly conceal the sticks, so as not to show the current standing of the team.) Gaming frequently goes on until dawn, or until one side is psychically or financially depleted. Sometimes stakes can run into the hundreds of dollars.

ball field. The dances of this region, still held today, are the Jumping, the White Deerskin, and the Brush dances.

In the days before the Europeans, the villages were small, independent communities seldom numbering more than 200 persons, with related peoples speaking related languages, and practicing their religions, mostly honoring the cycle of World-Renewal. Small villages that exist for long periods of time without authoritarian governance are the sign of a culture that can live in peace and trust within. Here, it was so.

Governance was through tribally-selected leaders or by common consent — one reason why U.S government-dictated tribal councils are not felt to be within tradition. In the northwest, display of wealth was a fairly common practice, with ornaments and household goods conferring elevated status.

There was always plenty of work to do: building boats, making baskets or tools, fishing and hunting, cleaning the catch, smoking the meat, preparing the hides, cutting wood for homes and fires. Though these cultures only practiced farming on a very small scale, planting the necessary herbs, grasses, and foods was important, too. The earth provided sustenance, but also time for relaxation.

Quiet times, fishing or by firelight, give the right aura for storytelling, time to exchange the stories, the myths, and the legends of culture. The legends of Coyote were very popular, because he was such an unpredictable character — the trickster: humorous, sly, deceptive, lecherous. Coyote twisted the expected world, and everyone laughed.

Games included a kind of hockey, archery, dice, and the insightful hand (or "grass") games. This game, with variations, is played in every Indian community in California, and much of the rest of North America as well. The drumming and singing of ancient traditional songs with the game is fascinating, as is following the game itself, which is usually played at Big Times.

THE RESERVATIONS & RANCHERIAS OF NORTHWESTERN CALIFORNIA

HUGGING THE ROCKY, WIND SWEPT, PINEY COAST OF THE NORTHWESTERN CORNER of California is the **Smith River Rancheria**. The **Tolowa** people have occupied this land for many centuries, and live in the quiet, scenic 160-acre rancheria and in the nearby communities. The Howonquet Tolowa and Yurok burial ground is here, disturbed only by the ocean wind on surf and pines. A short distance away is the historic Shaker Church of 1929, one of the few in the West. The Smith River is the site of a twice-yearly salmon run, which is held sacred by these people. Dances are held for the Indian community (the public is invited) the first week of August and the 21st of December (solstice).

Smith River Rancheria is reached from Hwy. 101 on the Mouth of Smith River Rd., right on South Indian Rd. in a loop to North Smith River.

About 35 miles south of Smith River, through the redwoods along U.S. 101, where the Klamath River pours into the Pacific, one encounters the exceptionally beautiful **Yurok Reservation**. Dotting the north slope is the ancient Yurok fishing village of Requa, populated largely by non-Indians today, but still within the reservation, which extends for one mile on each bank of the Klamath upriver to the Hoopa Reservation. The present Reservation administrative center is in the town of Klamath. Across the river lies a small Yurok rancheria, where smoked salmon is made for the tribe. (Some may be for

sale along the highway.) (Campsites available.)

The upriver portion of the reservation, approachable only from the south along Hwy. 96, is largely inaccessible, and is an exceptionally secluded place, with much of the land a nearly pristine reserve. The villages along the river have been in their places for thousands of years, nearly undisturbed, though nearby lumber companies have, in the past, induced authorities to allow some severe lumbering.

> **THE VILLAGES ALONG THE RIVER HAVE BEEN IN THEIR PLACES FOR THOUSANDS OF YEARS, NEARLY UNDISTURBED.**

Ancestral Yurok lands extended along the coast south of the Klamath also, as far south as Trinidad; today Yurok live at Big Lagoon Rancheria (private) and the **Tsurai (Cher-Ae) Rancheria** (State Landmark plaque **838**), which sit on ancient village sites. Perched on a bluff overlooking Trinidad Head, Tsurai offers a modern clinic for the people's health, and for recreation, modern bingo. To get an excellent feeling of life as it was in a Yurok village, visit the authentic replicas of ancient structures constructed by the Yurok and California State Parks people at **Sumeg, Patricks Point State Park**. (See also p. 26.)

The Yurok Reservation extends along the Klamath River from Requa to Weitchpec, but is accessible only to Klamath Glen from Hwy. 101 on the lower portion. Access to the upper portion is from Hwy. 96 to Johnsons or via Bald Hills Rd. from Redwood National Park on Hwy. 101 to Martins Ferry. (The Bald Hills are a result of a traditional Indian practice of the controlled burning of certain areas to maintain grassy meadows that attract deer and elk.)

▲ *The July 4th Hoopa All-Indian rodeo is an event well calculated to stimulate and entertain the audience.*

▲ *The Tolowa burial ground on the Smith River Rancheria is a quiet place suited for meditation and contemplation.*

▲ *The Hupa Tribal Administration building has the smooth curve of a roundhouse. Though quite large, it blends artfully with the surrounding hills.*

▲ *The Karuk Orleans tribal community hall is built on land acquired by grant to and purchase by the local Karuk tribal members.*

Camping is available at several sites in Six Rivers National Forest above Weitchpec.

Sumeg in Patricks Point State Park on U.S. 101 five mi. N of Trinidad is an authentic Yurok area. Camping is available.

Tsurai (Trinidad Rancheria) is situated 1 mi. south of Trinidad on the coast bluff road, accessed from the Trinidad Exit off Hwy.101.

From the forests and creeks along the Trinity River to its confluence with the Klamath, U.S. Army troops, in the 1860s, herded the populations of at least four peoples into a big twelve-mile square. The people were **Chimariko**, **Whilkut**, **Chilula**, and **Yurok**. This area was already home of the **Hupa** people, and was given the name **Hoopa Reservation**. The very size of the reservation affords some support of the people from its natural resources — forestry, fishing, and some farming.

Hoopa is a most interesting place: the steep canyon and quiet flats of the Trinity, green mountains covered with conifers, green valleys lined with many other trees, stores, a bingo hall, rodeo grounds, an informative museum of the valley peoples, a tribal center so integrated into the environment that it is hard to find, an old U.S. Army fort (now used by the BIA and other agencies), and the most ancient villages that I know of in North America. Remnants of some ten of the original thirteen Hupa villages remain, some restored. At least one religious site has been in continuous use for 5,000 years. These attractions will surely entice you to visit this place to know the Northern California Indian cultures of today and of ancient times.

Hoopa Valley Reservation is on State Hwy. 96, about 35 miles east of Eureka, along the spectacular Trinity River gorge.

As you travel up the Klamath River, the countryside becomes gradually drier. It is warmer in summer, colder in winter, and you come into the ancestral lands of the **Karuk** people. The Karuk once occupied the land and mountains along the Klamath from near Orleans to

Seiad. After the devastation by miners in the last century uprooted most of the people from their original homes, many moved up the tributaries into former Shasta country.

Very few Karuk reservation lands exist, but new ones are being added, mostly for residences. A tiny 7-acre plot in Orleans (at the bridge) was bought by the Karuk people themselves; further up, in Happy Camp, the strikingly beautiful architecture of the tribal center of the **Karuk Tribe of California** overlooks the center of town. From here the tribe administers scattered parcels of Karuk land in Orleans, Somes Bar, Forks of Salmon, Quartz Valley, Seiad Valley, Scott Valley, and Yreka.

The land of the *Shasta* peoples of the middle Klamath region stretched from Mt. Shasta, north to Ashland, Oregon, and west to Seiad Valley, and centered on what is now Yreka. Although these people have essentially no reservation land today, they do indeed exist, and are organized as the **Shasta Nation** in Yreka.

Coastal lands from Trinidad to Cape Mendocino along the expansive and fertile deltas of the Eel and Mad Rivers were occupied by the **Wiyot** people. This group has been among the most severely dispossessed of all the peoples of this region; it was the Wiyots, along with two other groups, who suffered the massacre on Indian Island in 1860. A small portion of Wiyot land remains at the **Table Bluff Rancheria**, and is in the process of being expanded. Table Bluff is located on a parcel of tableland above a Pacific Ocean beach; the fierce winds are partly mitigated by windrows of a few trees. The homes here are older; nevertheless, the community survives and soon will occupy new and (hopefully) better homes. A small number of Wiyot people also reside at the Blue Lake and Rohnerville Rancherias.

Table Bluff Rancheria is approached via Hookton Rd. Exit off U.S. 101, 10 mi. S of Eureka (direction of Humboldt Co. Beach Park) to Indian Reservation Rd.

On the highway map, U.S. 101 makes a big loop around a large patch of forest between Leggett and Rohnerville in Mendocino County. Only one dirt road traverses this wild, nearly unsettled, mountainous region. Yet, in the last century, whites swept the region's Indian population nearly to extinction — the land of five small tribes: the **Mattole**, **Nongatl**, **Sinkyone**, **Lassik**, and **Wailaki**. A very few Sinkyone individuals survive; several Wailaki families survive in the **Round Valley Reservation** where they were driven, many miles to the east.

One other northwestern group related to those above persists — the **Cahto** people, on the **Laytonville Rancheria**. The Cahtos are not a coastal people, but rather live in the hills and oak savannahs of the Coast Range; nevertheless, they are related by language to their more northern Athapaskan neighbors. This little enclave is rather typical of the rancherias of this region — a small, but cohesive group, they have built a roundhouse of cedar in the center of the reasonably comfortable homes of the rancheria, and the quietest spot in this quiet place is the small burial ground on the hill.

Laytonville Rancheria lies 2 mi. W of Laytonville just S off Branscomb Rd.

> REMNANTS OF TEN ORIGINAL HUPA VILLAGES REMAIN, ONE RELIGIOUS SITE HAS BEEN IN CONTINUOUS USE FOR 5,000 YEARS.

WE ARE A SOVEREIGN PEOPLE.

Our Grandfathers fought to keep us free.

We have abandoned our gift and our responsibilities for the easy life and empty promises.

Now we rededicate our lives to those yet unborn.

—from a mural on the Hoopa Reservation High School

NORTHEASTERN CALIFORNIA

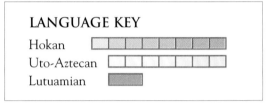

LANGUAGE KEY

Hokan

Uto-Aztecan

Lutuamian

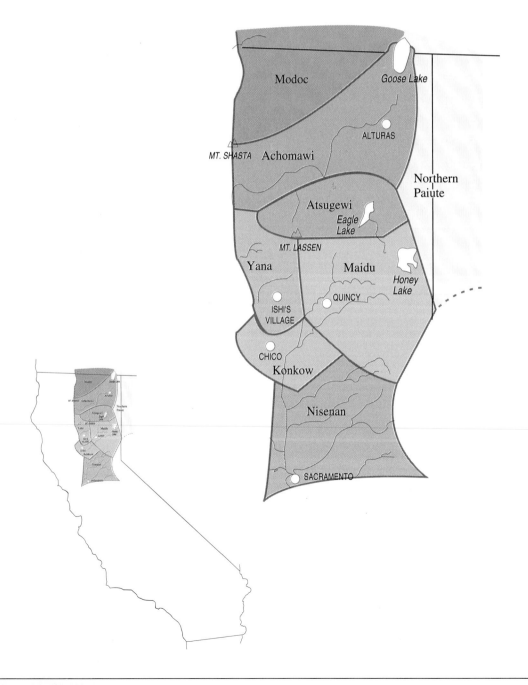

Modoc

Goose Lake

ALTURAS

MT. SHASTA   Achomawi

Northern
Paiute

Atsugewi

Eagle
Lake

MT. LASSEN

Yana

Maidu

Honey
Lake

QUINCY

ISHI'S
VILLAGE

CHICO

Konkow

Nisenan

SACRAMENTO

THE PEOPLES	THE RESERVATIONS & ORGANIZATIONS	

Hokan Speakers [b]
Pit River Tribes: *Achomawi, Aporige, Astarwawi, Atsuge (Hat Creek), Atwamsini, Hammawi, Hewisedawi, Ilmawi, Itsatawi, Kosalextawi, Madesi*

Tribal Center (Burney), Alturas, Lookout, Montgomery Creek, Big Bend, and Roaring Creek Rancherias, Likely Cemetery, and X-L Ranch Reservation

[b] *Hokan is an ancient language group found in diverse areas of the state, and is distantly related to groups of northern and central Mexico.*

Yana-Yahi

(none)

Penutian Speakers [d]
Maidu

Greenville, Berry Creek, Enterprise Rancherias
organizations: in Susanville and Taylorsville

[d] *Penutian languages probably arose in California; they are found largely in the central and northern parts of the state.*

Konkow (Northwestern Maidu)

Mooretown Rancheria, Chico Burial Ground

Nisenan (Southern Maidu)

Auburn Rancheria

Shoshonean Speakers [e]
Northern Paiute

Fort Bidwell Reservation, Cedarville, Susanville Rancherias

[e] *Shoshonean is one of a large family of Uto-Aztecan languages spoken in the Great Basin, in eastern and southern California, by the Comanches, and by the Aztecs of Mexico. (See also p. 111.)*

Lutuamian Speakers [f]
Klamath & Modoc

Tribal Center (Chiloquin, Oregon)
no California trust land

[f] *The Lutuamian language family is found mostly to the north — in Oregon and eastern Washington.*

▲ *Ishi's cave, Mt. Sutro, San Francisco. Ishi, a Yana of the forests below Mt. Lassen, was probably the last California Indian who chose to live completely separate from the white culture. Under extreme pressure by local ranchers, who considered his group wild prey, to be hunted, he surrendered in an Oroville corral in 1911. He was brought by Alfred Kroeber to the University of California Museum of Anthropology (then in San Francisco), from which he sought out this rockshelter in Sutro Forest for occasional refuge. Ishi died in 1916 of tuberculosis.*

THE PEOPLES OF NORTHEASTERN CALIFORNIA

THE PEOPLES OF NORTHEAST CALIFORNIA LIVE ON THE GREAT, HIGH PLAIN CALLED THE MODOC Plateau that extends from the Oregon border south to Mt. Lassen. There the Plateau wrinkles into rugged forms, becoming the northern Sierra Nevada. In the north, the Plateau is punctured with the evidence of volcanic activity — Shasta and Lassen and a dozen more volcanic peaks, lava beds, cinder cones, and spines of rounded rock pushing up from under the earth.

The meandering streams are sometimes trapped by the moving rock, ponding in lakes and bogs. It is icy in winter, hot in summer, and very, very dry in the east. Inevitably, the lifestyles of these peoples would be different from those of the northwest, or the torrid Central Valley. Some of these peoples dwelt on the downslopes of the Plateau and the Sierra, finding better sustenance in the warmer climates facing the Central Valley. This environment, of the **Yana**, **Konkow**, and **Nisenan**, was intermediate between that of the high Sierra and the Central Valley.

Possibly the most famous Indian of California, Ishi, was from the Yahi tribe of Yana, and lived along the creeks that flowed from the Mt. Lassen area. (My readers are urged to read about this daring, capable, and likeable person (ref. 10). Since I walk his paths to my work every day, thoughts of his existence are always with me.)

Nature provides, but in this climate, it was necessary to work a bit harder. Fish were plentiful (until dams); deer, antelope, elk, and birds were abundant; tubers, acorns, and seeds were major food items, as were, yes, crunchy roasted grasshoppers. (We eat shrimp, don't we?) Grizzlies roamed about, but were avoided, seldom hunted, and were regarded as animals worthy of the greatest respect. The Bear Dance of the **Maidu** makes this quite clear — you soothe the bear in the dance, hoping that your attitude will keep you safe and in this giant's good graces, should you encounter one on the trail.

> THE FIERY CONES OF SHASTA AND LASSEN MUST HAVE BEEN RELIGIOUSLY INSPIRING WHEN THEY ERUPTED.

An excellent grade of obsidian (volcanic glass) for arrow points was so plentiful that it was traded all over the West.

The people lived in a variety of dwellings — warm, conical tipis made of cedar bark or slab strips in the forested areas; more temporary brush shelters in those parts where the summer sun must be shaded and the living was nomadic, following the deer. In the warmer places, a semi-subterranean, mud-over-sapling frame home was more comfortable.

The fiery cones of Shasta and Lassen must have been religiously inspiring when they erupted, and their continuously-seething hot springs are proof that Mother Earth is alive even when they are dormant. Both snowy peaks are sacred to the many tribes which bore them in their vision daily.

On the eastern edge of California, the **Paiute** and **Shoshone** peoples carry a vision somewhat different from the peoples of the forest-enclosed west,

whose orientation is more toward *earth* and *mother*. Their vision was toward *sky* and *father*; they spent their days and nights on the open plains.

The Paiute people are the source of an unusual religion which originated in the Great Basin culture. The initiation of the Ghost Dance was from Wodziwob, of the Walker River Reservation, Nevada, in 1870. A later version was practiced in 1890 by Wovoka, near Yerington, Nevada. They envisioned the Ghost Dances at times when Indian causes had been completely crushed by the white man. One of several beliefs of Ghost Dance followers was that a certain shirt design could be made impervious to bullets, and that the white man would disappear if the dances were performed appropriately. Tragically, a test was made of the claims — and failed. Even so, elements of the Ghost Dance spread to many of the California Kuksu tribal dances (see p.21) and remain with them to this day.

▲ *Top: The banner of striped maple with the bearskin says that the bear is "in residence"—ready for the Maidu Bear Dance. On the last day of the gathering, a member of the tribe becomes the bear. All the attendees dance in a circle around the arena, stroking the dancing bear with switches of fragrant mugwort (wormwood) while the bear randomly visits individuals, humorously trying to make them nervous. Finally, the bear departs, hopefully in a good mood. (Bear Dances of other tribes are usually somewhat more serious than this one.)*

◀ *Bottom: This stone building was once part of the Fort Bidwell Indian School. when the school was closed, it was turned into residences.*

THE RESERVATIONS & RANCHERIAS OF NORTHEASTERN CALIFORNIA

THE NORTHEAST CORNER OF CALIFORNIA, LIKE THE NORTHWEST, IS INDIAN COUNTRY; THE spacious **Fort Bidwell Reservation** (State Landmark **430**) of the **Paiute** people is located here. Once a people of the desert, the Paiute were obliged long ago to settle into a farming and ranching existence, with some employment in the lumbering industry of the Warner Mountains. This range manages to scrape enough moisture from passing storms to water a sizeable forest above the reservation, and feeds irrigating streams that aim toward Alkali Lake, but seldom arrive. The reservation is home to some 175 persons, with a mix of old and new buildings, the oldest being an Indian school of 1897. The vistas are superb, the summer gold and green alfalfa is stored in picturesque wooden barns, and you might think you were in Colorado.

Fort Bidwell Reservation is located at the end of the paved road north from Cedarville (St. Hwy. 299).

Visits to the six scattered parcels of the X-L Ranch and the six small rancherias of the **Pit River Tribes** of Modoc County, or even the Tribal Center or medical clinics in Burney would be instructive only through observing the high plateau countryside of the Pit River peoples. The Ft. Crook Museum in Fall River Mills does present some Pit River history. By the way, the Pit River people used to trap deer by digging and camouflaging a pit — hence the name.

> WITH 60 MEN AND WOMEN, KINTPUASH (CAPTAIN JACK) HELD OFF 600 ARMY TROOPS FOR 4 MONTHS IN THESE LABYRINTHINE LAVA BEDS.

On a visit to the Visitors Center of **Lava Beds National Park** (off St. Hwy. 139) you will find a sensitive, accurate account of the tribulations and trials of **Modoc** leader Kintpuash (Captain Jack) and his group of Indian resisters against white incursions. With 60 men and women, he held off 600 Army troops for four months in these labyrinthine lava beds. He was eventually defeated and hanged; many of the tribe were shipped to Oklahoma. Here, too, are ancient Modoc abstract pictographs and the largest group of petroglyphs in California. (See p. 24 for more information.)

A revived Modoc people have lately begun to emerge from their seclusion to honor the deeds of Kintpuash and their past. Honoring ceremonies are held during the second weekend in July, in the section of the Park now known as "Captain Jack's Stronghold."

The **Maidu** people and their closest linguistic cousins, the **Konkow** and **Nisenan**, have few trust lands to call their own, but this group of people does have a very strong survival instinct. The Maidu near Lake Almanor continue to expand their operations in the neighborhood of the **Greenville Rancheria**. Their small tribal center is a center for the tribal supervision of the care for their people — meals, medical care, administrative details, even the perpetuation of the language. A family of the tribe also sponsors an annual Bear Dance in the summer. Details may be obtained at the tribal office.

▲ *The Pit River people have long contested the Pacific Gas & Electric Company's expropriation of a huge block of their lands for timber and hydroelectric projects. This trailer on the disputed land is at least symbolic of their protest.*

▲ *A Maidu cemetery in the Indian Valley of Plumas County. Most traditional Indian burial grounds use few, if any markers.*

The Greenville Rancheria tribal offices can be found on Old Taylorsville Rd., 4 mi. E of Greenville.

Not a place to be visited yet, the formerly remote **Berry Creek (Tyme Maidu) Rancheria** has acquired new land and has ambitious plans to erect a large center on Hwy. 162 near Oroville. Cruise by in the future. This is one of the examples of the powerful efforts of the Indians of this state to see that their people are better provided for.

In 1958, some history and prestige were lost when the **Auburn Rancheria** council was given bad counsel to force their own termination from trust status. (See p. 68.) Since that time their economic status has remained at a very low ebb, though most of the original families still own their former property allotments. Strong legal efforts are in the works to return the land to trust status and secure the resultant benefits. Bad times or not, the people are very active in Indian affairs in the Auburn area — in seeing to their people's nutrition, health, and rights, as well as supporting a young dancers' group. The tribe also maintains a cemetery, formerly a cremation ground, a short distance from the rancheria. The majority of the homes are aging, and wood is commonly used for heating and cooking. On the grounds is an historic Protestant church. Indian life here appears suspended thirty-five years in the past.

Auburn Rancheria is about 2 mi. S of Auburn center, at Indian Rancheria Rd. on Auburn-Folsom Rd.

Shield (protection) & Fallen Shield Modoc petroglyphs Lava Beds National Park

MODERN STRUCTURES

The twentieth century rush of life and the upheavals of Indian existence forced a transient and mobile way of life upon the Native population, especially the men who were required to leave home for work for long periods of time. At least they had a small parcel to occasionally return to, where they might erect a simple shack or park a trailer, even in the 1930s.

In the past decade government grants have enabled many of the people to purchase "mobile" homes, to attach to their earlier inadequate places, or to live in separately. Other Department of Housing and Urban Development grants have allowed construction of larger tracts of homes. The ugly prize goes to a rectangle of tiny, boxy sweat houses jammed into the Rincon Reservation. However, most new homes are fairly substantial houses including basic services, erected with care in attractive settings, often on newly-acquired land, such as the **Robinson** and the **Rumsey Rancherias** (near Clear Lake) or two-story homes on the **Santa Rosa Rancheria,** or single-family homes on the **Round Valley** and the **Chemehuevi Reservations.** Strikingly unique are the new homes with high windows set to gather in the winter sun under the soaring White Mountains in the mile-high valley of the **Benton Paiute Reservation.**

Tribal centers and community buildings with striking architectural designs are an especially welcome discovery in an age of mediocrity. Extraordinarily pleasing designs, with careful consideration of tribal tradition and natural features can be seen in the **Hupa Tribal Hall,** the **Karuk Tribal Center** (Happy Camp), the **El-em Community Center** (Clear Lake), the **Bishop Reservation Tribal Center,** the **San Manuel Tribal Hall,** the **Campo Tribal Center,** and the **Quechan Tribal Hall** (Fort Yuma), among others. I wish I could say the same for the numerous bingo palaces sprinkled around the state. Most look like partly-dressed warehouses, notable exceptions being **Cache Creek** (Rumsey Rancheria) and **San Manuel.**

▲ *Big Sandy (Auberry) Rancheria in the Sierra foothills has erected a modern tribal center that inspires a stirring vision of the natural world.*

▲ *The Karuk Tribal Center at Happy Camp is a fine example of the artistic architecture frequently seen in more recent Indian administration buildings.*

CENTRAL COAST
& CENTRAL VALLEY

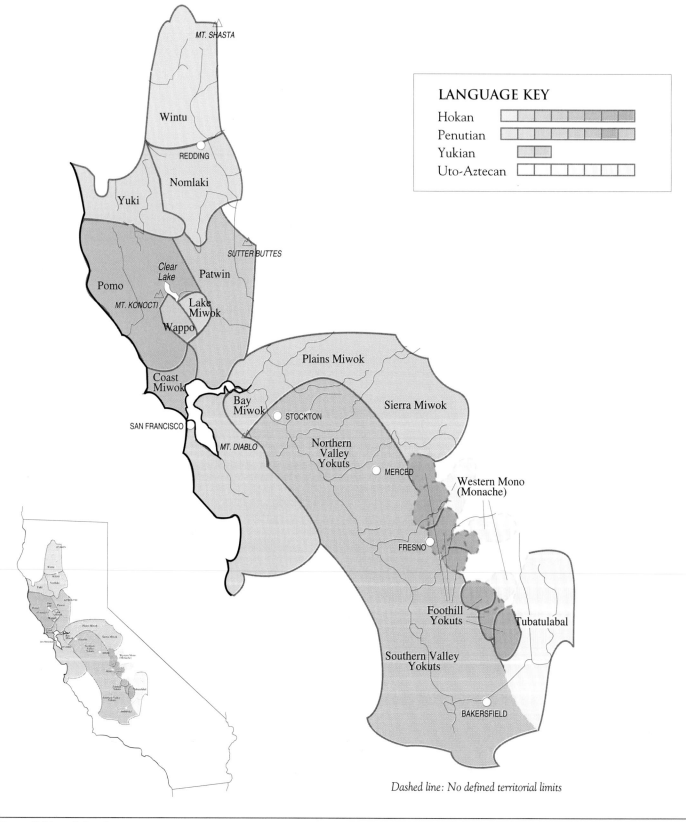

LANGUAGE KEY

Hokan
Penutian
Yukian
Uto-Aztecan

MT. SHASTA

Wintu

REDDING

Nomlaki

Yuki

Clear
Lake

SUTTER BUTTES

Patwin

Pomo

MT. KONOCTI

Lake
Miwok

Wappo

Plains Miwok

Coast
Miwok

Bay
Miwok

STOCKTON

Sierra Miwok

SAN FRANCISCO

MT. DIABLO

Northern
Valley
Yokuts

MERCED

Western Mono
(Monache)

FRESNO

Foothill
Yokuts

Tubatulabal

Southern Valley
Yokuts

BAKERSFIELD

Dashed line: No defined territorial limits

THE PEOPLES

RESERVATIONS AND ORGANIZATIONS

Penutian Speakers [d]
Wintun family:
Wintu, Nomlaki, Patwin

Round Valley Reservation*, Redding*, Cortina, Grindstone Creek*, Colusa (Cachil Dehe), Rumsey Rancherias; *organizations:* four groups in Redding area, No'r-El-Muk Band (Hayfork)

[d] *Penutian languages probably arose in California; they are found largely in the central and northern parts of the state.*

Miwok languages:
Coast and Lake Miwok

Middletown Rancheria; dedicated land: Kule Loklo (Point Reyes)
organizations: Bodega Bay Tribe, Tomales Bay Tribe

Plains Miwok

Wilton Rancheria

Sierra (N, Central, S) Miwok

Sheepranch, Shingle Springs, Jackson, Buena Vista, Tuolumne, Chicken Ranch Rancherias; Ahwahnee Village (Yosemite); dedicated land: Chaw-Se (Amador Co.);
organizations: Ione Band (Amador Co.) Calveras Co. Miwoks, Mariposa Co. Council

Ohlonean (Costanoan)

Indian Canyon (Mutsun Ohlone); *organizations:* Muwekma Tribe, Pajaro Valley Council

Yokuts (several bands)

Picayune, Table Mountain, Santa Rosa (Táchi) Rancherias, Tule River Reservation*, Wassama Roundhouse (Chukchansi Tribal office);
organizations: Chukchansi Tribe (Oakhurst), Choinumni Tribe (Fresno), Wukchumni Tribe (Fresno Co.)

more...

THE CENTRAL COAST
AND CENTRAL VALLEY (continued)

THE PEOPLES

RESERVATIONS AND ORGANIZATIONS

Hokan Speakers [b]
Pomo family - 7 languages
Northern, Northeastern, Eastern, Central, Southeastern, Southern, Kashaya

Sherwood Valley (Mato, N), Potter Valley (Balo-Kay, N), Redwood Valley (Kacha, N), Coyote Valley (N), Scotts Valley (N), Guidiville (N), Pinoleville (Yamo, N), Yo-Ka-Yo (C), Hopland (Shokowa-ma, C), Graton (S), Manchester-Point Arena (Bóya, (C), Dry Creek (S), Cloverdale (Khalanhko, S), Upper Lake (Matuku, E), Stewarts Point (Kashaya), Robinson (E), Big Valley (E), El-ém Rancherias (SE); Stonyford community (private land, NE)

[b] *Hokan is an ancient language group found in diverse areas of the state, and is distantly related to groups of northern and central Mexico.*

Yukian Speakers [g]
Yuki & Coast Yuki

Round Valley Reservation*

Huchnom

(none)

Wappo

Alexander Valley burial ground

[g] *Yukian languages are a small group found only in this region.*

Shoshonean Speakers [e]
Western Mono (Monache)

North Fork, Big Sandy, Cold Springs Rancherias; Tribal Center (North Fork); Tule River Reservation*;
organization: Dunlap Band

[e] *Shoshonean is one of a large family of Uto-Aztecan languages spoken in the Great Basin, in eastern and southern California, by the Comanches, and by the Aztecs of Mexico. (See also p. 111.)*

Tubatulabal

Tule River Reservation *

*Shared with other groups

▶ *A dancer at Kule Loklo.*

▲ *Grindstone Creek Rancheria roundhouse (Nomlaki), the oldest in California, built in the late 1800s.*

PEOPLES OF THE CENTRAL COAST AND THE CENTRAL VALLEY

THE CENTRAL VALLEY IS OFTEN SPOKEN OF AS IF IT WERE MUCH THE SAME FROM REDDING TO Bakersfield. It isn't, but there are some similar features. It is flat, it is hot in summer, it is rimmed by mountains, and its early Indian peoples spoke similar languages (see Map I, p.25). The expectation is that a similar topography would engender similar ways of living, but that is only partly true.

In this section, we will consider also the people living in an adjacent, but different geography at the margins of the Valley — the peoples of the Central Coast Range, and those peoples whose ancestral lands are in the foothills of the Sierra Nevada.

The similar customs practiced by all these peoples has been called the Central California Culture. In the Coast Range a number of broad, flat valleys encouraged a very settled lifestyle. Through each valley courses a creek or river, sustaining oak flats, grasslands, and the conifer trees of the nearby mountains. Even in summer, the mountains slowly release their stores of winter-gathered water. Game, birds, and fish were abundant. The topography is sufficiently rugged that tribes stayed put in their villages, or moved only short distances.

For the people in the Central Valley, the flat valley floors of both the Sacramento and the San Joaquin Rivers became unfriendly places twice a year — when flooded with the winter rains, and when the mountain snows melted

in June. Early explorers describe the floods as an inland sea, a huge marsh; this made winter "quarters" on higher ground a must. In summer, the rivers quieted into a wetland maze, and the hunting grounds spread over the entire valley. Pursuing fish and game, hunters took to the water in small tule reed[6] canoes, similar to those of the Quechua of Peru.

Today, the Central Valley has been completely dammed, diked and dominated, so that muddy floods no longer regenerate the soil. Only tiny segments of the original marshes are preserved for bird migration — wetlands near Colusa, Los Banos, and Hanford — but without floods or salmon migration.

> EARLY EXPLORERS DESCRIBED THE CENTRAL VALLEY AS AN INLAND SEA IN WINTER. TODAY, THE VALLEY HAS BEEN DAMMED, DIKED, AND DOMINATED.

The peoples here, as in more northern regions, celebrated the World Renewal, and the dances of Kuksu and Hesi were integrated into the rituals. The dancers in these intricate rituals were at one time members of specially dedicated societies, and anyone wishing to advance in leadership positions in the tribe or medicine society was obliged to learn the rituals. The secrets of power were shared within the group, and with those holding similar positions in neighboring tribes, thus establishing intertribal religious ties. Such ties still exist today, but with somewhat diminished significance.

It is in this part of central California that the dancehouse or roundhouse is most often found as part of the religious rites. (The roundhouse is described on

[6] Tule is a marsh plant found throughout California, similar to cattails, but with the upper seed pod smaller and flower-like. Tule was used for everything from roofing to boats, and the shoots were a nutritious food.

Animal Tracks Pictograph, Miwok - Chaw-Se, Amador Co.

Pictograph
Miwok - Chaw-Se. Amador Co.

p. 26.) Building a roundhouse was not a simple matter, and not every village had one; they were (and are) found in the more permanent rancherias. The first requirements are dedication to build and to maintain the structure, but more important is the inspiration required to teach and perpetuate the traditions of the community with the young men and women. It was so then, and it is so today.

The *sweathouse*, not to be equated with the roundhouse, was also a common institution in these central California communities; almost every village had one. The sweathouse provided a means for social and community unity and organization, as well as being a healthy practice.

In these villages, tales of Coyote the Trickster were heard, as in the rest of the state. But Coyote's nature changes somewhat with the society. In the north, showing one's wealth was important, so tricks that irked the rich were popular. In central California, where wealth was not of great concern, Coyote's tricks were lustier and risqué. Here the stories tended to be less for "instruction" and more for entertainment; either way, stories always taught a moral.

I t was within these communities, especially the **Pomo** villages, that the art of basketweaving reached a level unsurpassed anywhere in the world. Baskets were made for collecting and transporting, for storage and for cooking, for water and for acorns, even for hats — most of them so well-decorated that they can be "art" pieces by themselves.

The weavers used both twining and coiling, some decorated with shells, beads, and feathers, others with intricate designs in multicolor, others remained simple and startling. They invented abstract designs, employed

designs with symbolism, designs that told stories, like rock art. Even the smallest of all baskets are made — one millimeter in diameter! It is a tribute to their excellence that this magnificent art of basketweaving has been passed down to weavers of today, and these beautiful baskets can command hundreds of dollars.

A longside the great Central Valley in the eastern foothills, more sedentary peoples made their homes. The foothills are well watered in the dry summer by rivers from the Sierra Nevada, which have carved "flats," wide spots in their valleys. These oak and willow-dotted flats made perfect settings for small villages of the **Miwok, (Western) Mono**, and **Yokuts** peoples, providing them with plentiful fish, game and plants. Acorns were a staple; deer, antelope, small rodents, seeds, green vegetables, and birds filled in their diets. Spacious cedar bark tipis grouped around the village center provided fairly permanent homes; in summer, cut-brush sun shelters were erected, much as tents are used today. Again, the roundhouse was frequently found in this region.

Village life was quite fixed, since the terrain prohibited much migration; hunting parties regularly tracked the Sierra mountains. Some bands (up to twenty in Yosemite Valley) lived in what is now national park land, and valued its incomparable scenic beauty. While protecting their homeland, the Yosemite dwellers were killed or displaced by the appropriately named Maj. James D. Savage.

T he flats also made good places for gold to collect, as the later miners found out, ultimately displacing almost all of the Natives. At the time of the

> IN THE NORTH, WEALTH WAS IMPORTANT, SO COYOTE'S TRICKS IRKED THE RICH. IN CENTRAL CALIFORNIA, COYOTE'S TRICKS WERE LUSTIER AND RISQUÉ.

gold rush, surviving inhabitants were pushed up into the hills into much less desirable land. Still, those people who were most adept at survival were able to maintain at least a minimal existence.

Summer in the Central Valley and its environs is brown; winter rains bring green, the inverse of much of the rest of North America. Nevertheless, spring brings salmon, fall brings harvest (acorn festivals) and anticipation of the coming green. **Tuolumne Rancheria, Kule Loklo (Point Reyes National Seashore), Chaw-Se (Grinding Rocks State Park), State Indian Museum (Sacramento), Santa Rosa Rancheria (Kings Co.),** and **Ya-Ka-Ama** all cele-brate the acorn harvest. (See Festivals Calendar.) In a sense, California and National Indian Day celebrations in September all celebrate the fall harvest, but not all with acorns. 🐎

▲ *Homes of the Wright brothers at Cortina Rancheria (Patwin). Although modern housing is available next door, Amos Wright prefers to summer in the old place.*

▼ *Large gatherings, such as the California Indian Days Powwow in Sacramento, offer excellent opportunities to watch and talk with master basket makers.*

BASKET WEAVING

Since basketry has long been recognized as an art, it is no surprise that a number of collections have been made. **Lowie Museum of Anthropology** at the University of California, Berkeley, has such a large and historic collection that only a fraction can be seen at any one time. While it is partially rotated, large portions of the collection seem to be forever hidden. A more visible collection, or rather set of collections, is displayed periodically at the **Riverside Municipal Museum**, covering the entire state by sections; another, at the **Bowers Museum** in Santa Ana is of great artistic importance. Seeing baskets being used in their settings, not just as objects under glass gives a better feel for them. For excellent diorama presentations, visit the **Sierra Mono Museum** in North Fork and **Yosemite Indian Village**. In Yosemite ancient baskets are actually in use by Indian Park naturalists.

THE RESERVATIONS & RANCHERIAS OF THE CENTRAL COAST & CENTRAL VALLEY

FROM THE FOOT OF MT. SHASTA TO THE FOOT OF MT. DIABLO, THE SACRAMENTO RIVER IS THE artery that connects three Wintun-language groups: the **Wintu** of the upper valley, the **Nomlaki** people of the central valley (Tehama and Glenn Counties), and the **Patwin** peoples of the lower valley to Suisun Bay.

Precious little along this 200-mile stretch of river is Indian country today, but a few spots remain. Examples: Clear Creek, flowing into the Sacramento at Redding, was the home of many Wintu, who were forced to flee or were massacred when the miners went for the gold, leaving an immense ruin of dredge tailings. The Wintu (and Pit River) **Redding Rancheria** at one time was whittled down to eight acres alongside that dredging; recent restoration of their land has increased their holdings to 38 acres, with a tribal inscription of over 2,000 members. In fact, one of the residents is a descendant of Ishi's tribe, Yana (obviously not extinct).

When Shasta Dam was finished, the workers' houses were scheduled to be demolished, but were later given over to a group of homeless Wintu. In 1989, the government decided that the houses were unfit, and with much turmoil expelled the Indian residents. Nevertheless, several Wintu organizations dedicated to the perpetuation of their tribal identities have emerged.

In 1854, a 25,000-acre reservation was established for the Nomlaki and neighboring tribes on some rather arid land on the east slopes of the Coast Range near Paskenta. The Indians worked it well, but in 1863, coveting this land, whites forced the people off it and removed them further west to the **Round Valley Reservation**, along with **Pit River**, **Wailaki**, **Konkow**, **Pomo**, and **Yuki** (whose ancestral land it was to begin with) in a massive roundup and "trail of tears."

The "reservation" is a pretty place, occupying the northern half of a five mile flat, round valley, fertile, well-enough watered, with mountain forests on all sides. But the one lumber mill operates only intermittently, no longer providing steady work. Access to Round Valley involves traveling 25 miles of a very curvy, scenic road. A medical clinic and a new tribal center try to provide the needed social services. Because the mix of Indian cultures has blurred tribal identities, and Christian churches have become established, a feeling of Indianness is somewhat missing, though the people have initiated a September Native American Cultural Celebration.

Round Valley Reservation is at the NE end-of-pavement of State Hwy. 162 (N of Willets).

In the east slope foothills of the Coast Range lie three other rancherias — two on creeks, one very dry with only a salty water well. On one of these, the **Grindstone Creek Rancheria (Nomlaki)**, stands the oldest extant roundhouse in California, built in 1874. Another, the **Rumsey Rancheria (Patwin)**, is close enough to Sacramento

> ON GRINDSTONE CREEK RANCHERIA STANDS THE OLDEST EXTANT ROUNDHOUSE CALIFORNIA, BUILT IN 1874.

▶ *Top: A small burial ground is the only extant remnant of the Chico Rancheria; it is maintained by members of the tribe.*

Bottom: Ft. Ross (from Russian Rossiya), in northwestern Sonoma County, was founded by the Russian-American Company (otter fur traders) in 1811. Construction and labor was provided, under contract with the company, by Kashaya Pomo Indians.

to derive a goodly income from bus- and carloads attracted to its Cache Creek Bingo. The third, the **Colusa Rancheria (Patwin)**, is home to both Colusa Bingo and an active roundhouse society. Colusa also borders the Sacramento River, but dikes seem to have protected its resources from the occasional floods. Although occupying only 273 acres, the setting is quietly rural, and makes a pleasant stop when driving along the Sacramento levees.

Rumsey Rancheria is located on State Hwy. 16 some 20 mi. W of Woodland (Yolo Co.).

Colusa Rancheria is about 3 mi. N of Colusa on State Hwy. 45.

Grindstone Creek Rancheria is situated at the confluence of Grindstone and Stony Creeks, 3 mi. N of Elk Creek on State Hwy. 162 (Glenn Co.)

P eppered around the region from the Pacific Coast to the center of the Coast Range near Clear Lake are 19 **Pomo** rancherias. A little background is in order. "Pomo" seems to have come from a word meaning approximately "the people from the red earth mine," mineralized red clay having been used for valuable red beads and as a food color for bread. The word was derived from the name of one village of this region. Within this region were no less than seven related languages — though as different from each other as English is from Swedish. (They are listed at the beginning of this section.)

The most remote of these villages is Kashaya, whose history involves a cordial relation with the Russian settlement at Fort Ross. The Kashaya people entered into an agreement with the Russian-American Company to do much of the Russians' work for them,

and established a satellite village (only now being archaeologically excavated) just outside the Fort Ross stockade. **Stewarts Point Kashaya Rancheria**, a secluded spot under redwoods, is a notably historical place, being the home of the late spiritual leader, the exceptional Essie Parrish, and the only site of two dancehouses. One, led by Ms. Parrish, is now closed out of respect to her.

Stewarts Point Rancheria is located about 8 mi. E of the coastal village of Stewarts Point (State Hwy. 1) on Stewarts Point-Skaggs Springs Rd. The roundhouses are OFF LIMITS to casual visitors.

Up the coast about 30 miles, the two villages of Point Arena and Manchester each have a (Central) Pomo Rancheria, peopled by branches of a Pomo family. At Manchester, alongside the tranquil Garcia River, stands a recently restored roundhouse, home for a very active group of Pomo dancers.

Inland, within twenty miles of the great Clear Lake, lie the majority of the (Northern, Eastern, Southeastern, Southern and Central) Pomo rancherias. For a good background on the Pomos of the region, consult the **Pomo Museum** in the north picnic grounds of Lake Mendocino. This most attractive and informative museum, built somewhat in the shape of a roundhouse, is staffed by local Pomo people, and occasionally, demonstrations of Pomo dance are held in the connecting amphitheater. The other source of information about the local Pomo peoples is the **Lakeport Museum**. A Pomo *balsa* (reed boat) can be seen here, along with displays of artifacts from the early peoples.

Pomo Museum is just E of Calpella, off Hwy. 20 in the Corps of Engineers-maintained Lake Sonoma Recreation Area.

Lakeport Museum is in the old County Courthouse, in the center of Lakeport.

Most of the rancherias of the area are quite small; many are simply rural or urban residential communities, although Robinson Rancheria's Kabatin

Bingo at Nice draws many people to its huge parking lot. To experience a sense of the Indian Country of this region, I recommend visits to two places. The first is the rather new **Coyote Valley Rancheria**, whose land replaces ancestral land drowned by Lake Mendocino. This place reflects the sense of community of a tribe, several families living in a quiet oak-shaded place with tribal center, ball field, and playground. A very dedicated group of young Pomo dancers is organized here, also.

The other place is the much, much older **El-em community**, at the edge of the ugly scar of the Sulphur Bank Mine, but under the towering cinder cone of Mt. Konocti. Who knows how long this place has been a village? Just over the hill is Borax Lake, on whose shores have been found arrow points nearly 10,000 years old!

The homes are of various ages, some recent, but the most striking feature of this community is the large dancehouse right in the center of the rancheria. Two years ago I lamented the passing of this spacious roundhouse, only to find another rise rapidly in its place. Erecting a structure of such exquisite carpentry takes much dedication, and the people here have it. I saw other facets of this allegiance at their "four-day dance" honoring the new building — dances in which the participants are obliged to commit themselves for four straight days and nights. I am told by the roundhouse captain (leader) that ritual dances are performed by many young people nearly every weekend, and that, as a result, the delinquency level here is quite low.

Coyote Valley Rancheria entrance is E on a road by Forsythe Creek, 1 1/2 mi. N of Calpella on U.S. Hwy. 101.

El-em Indian Colony is best approached on Sulphur Bank Rd., at the SE end of Clearlake Oaks on State Hwy. 20.

One tiny outlying (Northeastern) Pomo vestige is in Stonyford on private land (the tribe owned the only salt source for many miles); the three remaining (Southern) Pomo rancherias are to be found near the Russian River, between Ukiah and Healdsburg.

In ancestral Pomo country, with a mostly Pomo staff, is **Ya-ka-ama Indian Education and Development**. On once-disused land, in buildings abandoned by the government and occupied by some progressive Pomos at the time of the Alcatraz occupation, this active center sponsors a number of education programs for Indian peoples of all tribes: agricultural, horticultural, business and clerical skills, and programs in Indian ethnography. Under Ya-ka-ama sponsorship, Indian athletic and cultural events featuring dances, crafts, and foods attract hundreds of visitors throughout the year. This is probably the most popular gathering center for all the Indian peoples of the region.

> YA-KA-AMA IS PROBABLY THE MOST POPULAR GATHERING CENTER FOR INDIAN PEOPLES OF THE REGION.

Ya-ka-ama (Yah-keh-amah) is found N of Santa Rosa on River Rd. W 6 mi. to Trenton-Healdsburg Rd. Turn N for 1.5 mi. to Eastside Rd. Look to W of the wye for the Ya-ka-ama sign, 100 ft. Continue 1 mi. to the end.

Back to Clear Lake for a moment. This fount of pure, cold water, available year-round was attractive not only to the Pomo people. Groups found it necessary to seek water here in summer, and the territory of the **Lake Miwok** touched the lower tip of Clear Lake. (Their present-day remnant of land is in Middletown.) Because of the value of this natural resource, it is apparent why tribal group territories radiated out from here.

At the lower tip of otherwise over-developed Clear Lake, open space has fortunately been preserved in the form of the century-old Anderson Ranch,

◄ *Top: Coyote Valley Rancheria occupies a relatively new location, having been displaced from the lakebed of Lake Mendocino. Their cluster of homes is administered from this tribal center; several recreational facilities have been provided for all ages, from playgrounds to ball parks.*

Bottom: Ya-ka-ama Indian Education near Santa Rosa sponsors an all-Indian baseball tournament in the summer. Also offered are California Indian dances and food.

now **Anderson Marsh State Park**. Replicas of early Indian tule reed dwellings have been erected near the site of a lakeside village, and artifacts are displayed in the former ranchhouse. At least two gatherings are held annually at the Park, accentuating the early Indian and pioneer life of earlier times.

Anderson Marsh State Park is on State Hwy. 53, just E of Lower Lake on the SW bank of Cache Creek.

The **Wappo** people (the name is a transliteration of the Spanish *guapo*, handsome occupied a region between Clear Lake and the northern Napa Valley, including Mt. St. Helena. They were the northernmost group to suffer badly from Spanish depredations during the Mission Era. Not only did Gen. Vallejo use a mercenary platoon of Indians to wipe out any resistance to his takeover of their territory, but the missions, seeking fresh laborers ("converts"), also raided their villages. Today, little remains of their former lands, though several descendants are active in Indian affairs in the Healdsburg area. The Wappo still use an ancient burial ground in the Alexander Valley on a corner of a defunct rancheria; two other nearby rancherias have also disappeared in recent years, terminated after the last residents died or moved away.

Located on ancestral Patwin land is the all-tribal **D-Q University**, California's one college-level Native American educational institution. The name comes from unspoken spirit names for both North and Central American Native Americans. (Once, the University had an Hispanic component, but the government denied funds for that portion of the curriculum.) D-Q U specializes in social sciences, indigenous studies, sciences and humanities, agriculture, and "appropriate technology"

> **LOCATED ON ANCESTRAL PATWIN LAND IS D-Q UNIVERSITY, CALIFORNIA'S ONE COLLEGE-LEVEL NATIVE AMERICAN INSTITUTION.**

— the adaptation of new and old methods to facilitate modern living. All these subjects may be approached here in a manner which can be taught from a Native American perspective. Some 200 full- and part-time students take advantage of this unique program. D-Q U also sponsors monthly powwows and hosts several other Indian gatherings during the year.

D-Q U is just N of Road 31, 5 mi. W of Woodland, or 2 mi. E of I-505 (follow hwy. signs.)

From the Marin-Mendocino coast to the Sierra lies **Miwok** country. On the coast are the **Coast Miwok**; from Mt. Diablo to Placerville, **Bay** and **Plains Miwok**; from the Cosumnes River to the Fresno River in the foothills, three groups of **Sierra Miwok**. This area was blanketed with hundreds of villages — until Spanish disease and raiding decimated the western flank, and American diseases and miners nearly obliterated the easterners.

The Miwoks did not take their disintegration lightly. Of the Miwok Indian resistance fighters, three names stand out. Caught up in mission roundup expeditions, these three Miwok heroes proved ungrateful for mission treatment; they fled and fought courageously. Two have sardonically been given "saintly" place name status in Marin County — Marin and Quintin. The third was Estanislao (Stanislaus).

Of Coast Miwok country, very little is left in Indian hands. In both Bodega Bay and Tomales Bay small bands of Coast Miwok peoples have recently initiated tribal organization. **Kule Loklo** village in Point Reyes National Seashore is now dedicated to the use of the local Miwok people, as well as to neighboring Wappo and Pomo.

Of Plains Miwok, only a rancheria in Wilton (Sacramento Co.) with Indian-

Rattlesnake Petroglyph
Miwok - Chaw-Se, Amador County

A gallery of Indian dwellings of several eras:

Top Left: The plank house of the mid-1800s was a style built by both Indians and pioneers (Yosemite Indian Village)

Top Right: The earliest Gabrielino and Chumash dwellings of the Los Angeles area were tule reed domes. (This example was built especially for the Los Angeles Museum of Natural History by an elder.)

Bottom Left: From the early to mid-1900s, a one-room wooden place was often government issue. (Sheepranch Rancheria)

Bottom Right: This reasonably comfortable home of the 1930s style is Pomo-built. (Hopland Rancheria)

held private parcels is left, but in nearby Sloughhouse, a regional dance group drawn from Miwok residents is well-organized, and dances frequently.

The Sierra Miwok peoples have fared a bit better. The three groups (Northern, Central, and Southern) have six small rancherias among them, active tribal organizations in Ione and Mariposa, and two dedicated ceremonial and museum sites in **Chaw-Se** and **Ahwahnee Village** in Yosemite Park. **Chaw-Se Miwok Museum** is devoted to the **Sierra Miwok** culture — depicting daily life and explaining the myriad petroglyphs and grinding rocks just outside, as well as serving as a gallery for Native art shows twice yearly.

Ahwahnee Village is a part of the Yosemite Visitor Center centered on early Native life in the Park, portraying daily existence, including the making of acorn mush along with the making and use of baskets.

Within the Village are both a sweathouse and dancehouse, used regularly by the Miwok and Shoshone tribes of the region.

Of the six Sierra Miwok rancherias, two bring in some money through high-stakes bingo, one is so tiny that only one person can live there, one is strictly residential, and the remaining one, **Tuolumne Rancheria**[7], though remote, is very attractive and stirs with activity, a clinic, a well-used tribal hall, a roundhouse, and an acorn festival every September.

Chaw-Se Indian Grinding Rocks State Park is reached by going 8 mi. E of Jackson on State Hwy. 88 to Volcano Rd. in Pine Grove, then 1 mi. to the Park. Camping. Museum of Miwok Culture open 9-5, Wed.-Sun.

Ahwahnee Village is behind the Visitor Center of Yosemite National Park, and is staffed by local Miwok and Shoshone personnel who live in the Park, their ancestral home.

The Spanish called them **Costanoan**, people of the coast, because their observers tended to lump similar groups under one name. We know now that several groups of people lived in the region extending south from San Francisco Bay to Monterey Bay. Although we can give these tribes names, very few persons are left to claim them. The largest group of known descendants are the **Ohlone**, whose present tribal rolls number over 200.

(I say "known," because every so often, as pride in and knowledge of Native American background becomes of significance, people begin to step forward to publicly acknowledge their heritage. It has happened in Modoc, Marin and Los Angeles Counties, and slowly it happens in other places.)

The Ohlone people are hard-pressed to develop their tribal identity, as are all small, dispersed societies. Their only dedicated land is a burial ground, once an adjunct to the San José Mission; **Henry Cowell Redwoods State Park** (Felton) holds an annual **Ohlone Day** in October. Through the efforts of a few energetic spiritual and secular leaders, awareness of this people is being spread.

For an experience of the setting of the early Bay Area cultures, the **Coyote Hills Regional Park** cultural center and archaeological site near Fremont is highly recommended. A tule reed boat that actually floats is incorporated into displays of Miwok and Ohlone coastal marshlands and foothill culture.

Coyote Hills Regional Park is N of State Hwy. 84 at E end of the Dumbarton Bridge (Newark/Fremont).

California's most recent return of Indian country to Indian (and trust) control is Indian Canyon, a beautiful wooded valley in Mutsun Ohlone

[7] *In case you ever wondered, -umne is a Miwok suffix meaning "place of" (Mokelumne, Tuolumne, etc.).*

▶ *Top: A loghouse from Ft. Miller, used by the Army to subdue Indians of the Sierra foothills. It was transported to Rohner Park, Fresno, when the original site was flooded by Millerton Lake, adjacent to Table Mountain Rancheria.*

Bottom: Table Mountain Rancheria is named for this peculiar geological formation at the edge of the Central Valley.

country near Hollister. The land (private) was won back from government expropriation only after a struggle against a formidable bureaucracy. This triumph is as an excellent example of the on going Indian renaissance.

In the center of Mutsun country is Mission San Juan Bautista, site of one of the region's most visible Indian gatherings, the semi-annual **California Indian Market**. (See p.59.) Although the market draws Native Americans from nearly the entire hemisphere, neither the mission nor the town emphasize its Indian past.

Sprinkled along the river valleys on the west slope of the Sierra are several territories of the **Monache** (shortened to **Mono**). Their lands dovetailed with those of **Foothill Yokuts** to the west and south and of **Sierra Miwoks** to the north. Monache lifestyle was quite similar to the other two groups, since their ecological situation was almost identical; their language, however, is different, being related to Mono groups from the eastern side of the Sierras.

Today's Mono people are sprinkled about three rancherias and private homes along the Sierra front. The center of Mono tribal life is in North Fork at the **Sierra Mono Museum** and tribal offices. This museum is one of the best small museums for showing tribal life; dioramas portray artifacts *in use*, and the harmony of wildlife with Indian ways is emphasized. One of the most tranquil and enchanting experiences I have found in this entire region is the August **Sierra Mono Fair and Market** in North Fork. Camping is welcomed.

Big Sandy Rancheria in Auberry exemplifies the close Indian community in a rather secluded place. A small, very attractive tribal hall presides over the center of a circle of homes.

Sierra Mono Museum is 1 mi. from North Fork on Mamouth Pool Rd.

Big Sandy Rancheria is 4 mi. from Auberry (Fresno Co.) up Huntington Lake Rd. at Jose Basin Rd.

▲ *Profits from bingo operations can supplement government grants to construct better and more comfortable homes. These new homes are on the Santa Rosa Rancheria.*

▲ *The walls of the Painted Cave on the Tule River Reservation near Porterville possess some of the most elegant, though not entirely deciphered, painting of animals, spirits, symbols, and abstractions in the southern Central Valley region. The large "bearish" figure seen here is sometimes lightly, though respectfully, referred to as "Bigfoot" by Indians, but the figure probably represents a powerful spirit, since its shape is seen at many rock art sites in central California.*

Animals most frequently represented are bears, mountain sheep, deer, antelope, horses (after 1600s), fish, dolphins, snakes, lizards, turtles, birds (condors, eagles, hawks, quail), millipedes, and ants. Plants could be poppies, datura, leaves (or arrowheads), daisy-like flowers. Natural features are mountains, rain, clouds, streams, springs, trails, sun, moon, stars or planets. Spirits usually would possess anthropomorphic (human-like) features, but with special qualities for their attributes (hunting, protection, weather).

Occupying the largest territory, with the largest population of any California peoples, were the **Yokuts** groups, whose homelands extended over the Central Valley from Stockton to the Tehachapis and numbered some 40,000. They lived primarily along the San Joaquin River in summer and along other watercourses flowing from the Sierra the rest of the year. The daily lives of the various groups differed with the type of land they occupied, but all spoke similar dialects. Unlike other northern California peoples, they were not at first displaced by the gold miners, because the gold was not there. When the gold in the hills ran out, so did the miners, who turned to farming, seizing Yokuts lands, killing or driving the Native peoples away.

The displacement from the Valley was nearly complete. The one existing Valley community, **Santa Rosa Rancheria**, is relegated to a salty field, bordering on once-vast Tulare Lake. For decades, the people struggled to survive in this place, mostly as farm laborers. Within the last few years, their fortunes have turned better. New homes, a new tribal center, and nutritional help have been furnished, and, carefully distanced from the residences is a bingo palace. Santa Rosa sponsors a gathering in late August.

A few dozen Yokuts people still inhabit two other small rancherias, one of them with a bingo attractant (Table Mountain), but the majority of people were sent to the large **Tule River Reservation**, where they live today. In addition, a large number of Yokuts descendants live independently, not on reservation lands. Other Yokuts tribes, though without a land base, are organized in the Fresno area. In the town of Ahwanee a former farmhouse serves as an occasional Chukchansi Yokuts center. Adjacent is a Miwok burial ground and a fine, restored dancehouse, the **Wassama Roundhouse**, open to the public at the mid-July Gathering Day.

The California State Parks acquired the surroundings for all the local Indian people, and has dedicated the place to their use.

Santa Rosa Rancheria is located on 17th Ave. at Jersey Ave., 4 mi. S of Lemoore, Kings Co.

Wassama Roundhouse State Park is on Roundhouse Rd., 1/2 mi. N of Hwy 49 in Ahwahnee, Madera Co.

Tubatulabal people, a small group from the southern Kern River, basin no longer reside in that region. Their contemporary descendants live at the Tule River Reservation.

The **Tule River Reservation** is 54,000 acres of wonderful, nearly unspoiled Sierra mountain-to-valley scenery. The inhabitants have mostly clustered in a few areas where utilities are available, but several have ventured into the near-wilderness to live close to the nature of their ancestors. Yokuts were not the only peoples brought here. In major sweeps of the entire southern Valley and Tehachapi Mountains in 1859 and 1873, the Army deposited here remnants of **Mono, Tubatulabal, Kitanemuk,** and **Kawaiisu** peoples. Employment today is from seasonal lumbering (a mill was closed some years ago), some farming, and farm and oil field labor in the nearby Central Valley.

At one spot along the South Fork of the Tule River that courses through the reservation, the ancients painted the roof of a cave with astounding figures in colors that remain bright to this day. The **Painted Cave** may be visited with the services of a guide obtained at the tribal offices at the main village. Camping is not permitted on the reservation at this time; Forest Service campsites are available along the Middle Fork of the river.

Tule River Reservation is found at the end of Road J42 (off St. Hwy 190), 6 mi. E of Porterville. 🐎

▶ *Scenes like this bucolic river crossing abound on the scenic Tule River Reservation.*

EAST OF THE SIERRA DIVIDE

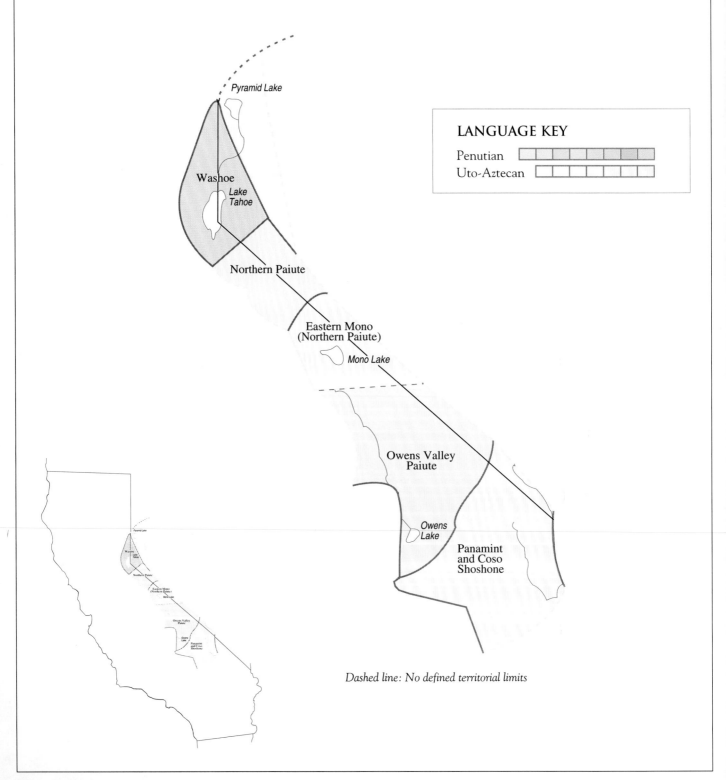

LANGUAGE KEY

Penutian

Uto-Aztecan

Pyramid Lake

Washoe

Lake Tahoe

Northern Paiute

Eastern Mono
(Northern Paiute)

Mono Lake

Owens Valley
Paiute

Owens Lake

Panamint
and Coso
Shoshone

Dashed line: No defined territorial limits

THE PEOPLES

THE RESERVATIONS & ORGANIZATIONS

Hokan Speakers [b]
Washo(e)

Alpine Washoe Reservation

[b] Hokan is an ancient language group found in diverse areas of the state, and is distantly related to groups of northern and central Mexico.

Uto-Aztecan Language Speakers [e]
Shoshonean:
Northern Paiute, Owens Valley Paiute
Eastern Mono, Shoshone (including Death Valley, Panamint, Coso)

Camp Antelope, Bridgeport Colony, Benton Paiute Res., Bishop Res., Big Pine Res., Fort Independence Res., Lone Pine Res., Timbi Sha Band (Death Valley Shoshone);
organization: Kern Valley Indian Council

[e] Shoshonean is one of a large family of Uto-Aztecan languages spoken in the Great Basin, in eastern and southern California, by the Comanches, and by the Aztecs of Mexico. (See also p. 111.)

Creation spirits, nr. Kawaiisu World Center,
Coso Shoshone, Inyo County

PEOPLES & RESERVATIONS
EAST OF THE SIERRA DIVIDE

WHEN THE MAPS WERE MADE DELINEATING CALIFORNIA, THE LINE WAS DRAWN JUST east of the Sierra mountain range, leaving only a tiny strip of the Great Basin within the State. This high, dry area presents a startling contrast to the Central Valley and the Sierra. We would rightly expect the life of the original peoples here to have been markedly different from those to the west.

The Shoshonean speakers of this region are descended from an extremely widespread group of fellow language speakers — from the Shoshone and Paiutes of the Great Basin to the Utes of Utah and Colorado and even to the Nahuatl (Aztecs) of Mexico. They are significant to California, because the peoples of this language group not only touch the Sierra on the east, but also occupy Indian country through the Owens Valley and almost the entire Mojave-Los Angeles Basin area.

The narrow strip of Great Basin in northeast California adjacent to Nevada is country of the **Northern Paiute**, a people whose lands extend into Oregon and Idaho as well as into central Nevada. Their California lands are included in the discussion of NE California peoples. (See p.78.) Other of these Shoshonean peoples whose lands are within California include the **Mono** (relatives of the Western Mono, above), whence we get Mono Lake; the **Owens Valley Paiute**; a portion of the **Western Shoshone** people (in the Panamints and

> THE LAND IS NOT DEVOID OF WATER; ONE MUST KNOW WHERE TO LOOK FOR IT, AND THE PAIUTES MADE FULL USE OF WHAT THERE WAS.

Death Valley); the **Kawaiisu** of the lower Kern River; and a portion of the **Southern Paiute**, including the **Chemehuevi** (a California Colorado River people). (These last three groups will be discussed in the next section.)

Generally, the Great Basin groups lived on land that, characteristic of high desert, is very warm in summer, and can be extremely cold in winter. The land is not devoid of water; one must know where to look for it, and the Paiutes made full use of what there was. One of their staple foods was fish from the many lakes and mountain streams. Piñon pinenuts was another staple, found on almost any mountain slope. (Paiutes still gather and sell these excellent nuts, indispensable for pesto sauce). Rabbit roundups were popular, and the deer and the antelope gave sustenance. The many marshes attracted migratory birds.

Clothing and dwellings were, of course, made from the available materials; the most interesting structures were very large ten-foot-high domed shelters made from the pliable willow trunks, covered with reed mats and/or skins. This design, not unlike Buckminster Fuller's modern domes, provides shelter from powerful desert winds, sand, and cold.

Artifacts of Indian activity in this region have been recovered from at least 5,000 B.C. Numerous beautiful rock art paintings are known throughout the desert region, though their meanings often remain uninterpreted. Some of these impressive carvings and paintings are to be found in California.

Indian Country

Of the few ceremonies that were practiced, an annual mourning for the dead, the "Cry" ceremony, is still observed in several communities. In addition, the Sun Dance and Bear Dance have been introduced from the Great Plains and Northern California tribes. It was with the Northern Paiute that the Ghost Dance had its origin.

One activity of the Great Basin peoples that impressed early visitors, and which continues into the present, is the ever-popular hand games (see p.74). Few Indian gatherings are held without avid Paiute participation.

South of the Northern Paiutes is the country of the **Washo(e)** (spelling variable), who inhabited the Lake Tahoe and upper Truckee River region. These people spoke a California Hokan language, and served as friendly trading intermediaries between the California and the Great Basin peoples. Trade consisted largely of salt from the salt lakes of Nevada, fish from Tahoe and Pyramid Lakes, and acorns (the Indian delicacy) from Maidu country. Today, Washoe land consists of the Alpine Washoe Reservation, a new site with fully-serviced homes and a tribal center near Markleeville, and a small settlement in Stewart (Carson City), Nevada.

The **Mono** people occupy a small corner of former Northern Paiute homelands. They have no reservation lands, but are well organized in Lee Vining as the Mono Lake Indian Community, and are seeking use of part of their traditional lands for ceremonial purposes.

OWENS VALLEY PEOPLE HARVESTED TWO BUGS: A HUGE PINE EATING CATERPILLAR AND BRINE FLY LARVAE... BOTH USED MUCH AS ASIAN CHEFS USE DRIED SHRIMP.

Further south, the **Owens Valley Paiute** people had set up an unusual society in an unusual place: a long, deep, and narrow valley. Somewhat like the peoples of northern California, geography confined to a certain space.

In this space they developed an irrigation system unique in California. Streams falling from the Sierra were diverted into communally-held meadows for seasonal watering of large crops of tubers. After harvest, crops were replanted. The Owens Valley people also harvested two crops of bugs. One was a huge pine-eating caterpillar, an insect with high protein value that keeps well when dried. The other was brine fly larvae which collected in drifts on the ancient Owens Lake. Apparently both foods were used much as Asian chefs use dried shrimp.

Other features that distinguished Owens Valley Paiutes from Great Basin peoples were the use of simple pottery and the use of a very large, 25-foot diameter semi-subterranean sweathouse (community house), something like the roundhouse of the north.

An excellent place to appreciate much of the early culture of this 80-mile-long valley is the **Paiute-Shoshone Museum and Cultural Center** on the **Bishop Reservation**, ornamented with startling designs, outstanding displays, and a crafts shop. On the reservation itself are many

▼ *An incomparable vista of the Santa Rosa Mountains from the Torres-Martinez Reservation, at the western edge of the Coachella Valley desert.*

historical older and newer buildings, in a magnificent setting. The Shoshone people here come from the Panamint valley and the desert country to the east of the Owens Valley.

North of Bishop, on the **Benton Paiute Reservation** unusual new homes are designed for sun-catching in winters that can be quite cold. Members of the tribe own a gas station/RV park with a restaurant noted for homemade soup at the main intersection, State 120 & U.S. 6. To the south, small reservations are found at the edges of Big Pine, Lone Pine, and Independence. Paiute-led horse pack trips to the Sierra may be hired at **Lone Pine Reservation**. The **Eastern California Museum** in Independence presents artifacts of early Paiute life.

Bishop Reservation is at the west end of Bishop on State Hwy. 168.

Benton Paiute Reservation is 1 mi. on Yellow Jacket Rd., just off State Hwy. 120 at Benton Hot Springs.

*The Kern Valley Indian Council currently represents landless **Kawaiisu, Tubtulabal, Coso Shoshone,** and **Yokuts** from this area (located in Kernville).*

The **Western Shoshone** people once occupied a large region from the Panamint Valley and Coso Range, through central Nevada, into northwestern Utah. In California their remnants are to be found in the above-listed Owens Valley reservations, in a tiny reservation in the arid Panamint Valley, and in **Death Valley National Monument** as the Timbi-Sha Shoshone Band who reside at aptly-named Furnace Creek. Their history is in part presented at the Visitors Center. 🐎

◀ *Left Top: New, environmentally-designed homes replace these two ancient clapboard houses on the Benton Paiute Reservation. Vistas of the White Mountains here are spectacular.*

◀ *Left Bottom: An old government building at Ft. Independence is put to better use as an Indian residence.*

▲ *Flag procession at the Tehachapi Powwow. This is an intertribal gathering of many Native Americans from the southern San Joaquin (Central) Valley, southern Sierras, and Los Angeles County areas.*

THE MOJAVE DESERT, COACHELLA VALLEY & COLORADO RIVER

LANGUAGE KEY
Hokan
Uto-Aztecan

Kawaiisu

Chemehuevi

Kitanemuk

○ VICTORVILLE

Mohave

Tataviam

Vanyume/Serrano

TWENTY-NINE PALMS

Cahuilla △ MT. SAN JACINTO

Salton
Sea

Cupeño

Quechan

○ YUMA
Cócopa

Dashed line: No defined territorial limits

THE PEOPLES

THE RESERVATIONS & ORGANIZATIONS

Shoshonean Language Speakers [e]
Shoshonean: Chemehuevi (Në-wë-wë)(Southern Paiute), Kawaiisu

Chemehuevi, Twentynine Palms, Colorado River Tribes Reservations

[e] Shoshonean is one of a large family of Uto-Aztecan languages spoken in the Great Basin, in eastern and southern California, by the Comanches, and by the Aztecs of Mexico.

Takic [h]
Kitanemuk, Tataviam, Cahuilla, Cupeño, Serrano-Vanyume

San Manuel, Soboba*, Cahuilla, Ramona, Santa Rosa, Los Coyotes, Torres-Martinez, Agua Caliente, Augustine, Cabazon, Morongo* Reservations

[h] Uto-Aztecan languages found in California comprise three major groups: the Shoshonean (Numic), the Takic and the Tubatubal. several Takic languages are poorly known, owing to extinction by the missions.

Hokan Speakers [b]
Mohave (Ha-mák-hava)†

Fort Mojave Reservation

[b] Hokan is an ancient language group found in diverse areas of the state, and is distantly related to groups of northern and central Mexico.

Quechan

Fort Yuma Reservation

*Shared with others.
†The spelling Mohave is used for the people; Mojave is used for geographical words.

▲ *Sunrise over Tahquitz (Mt. San Jacinto) from the Morongo Reservation (Riverside Co.).*
This massif ascends 10,800 feet abruptly from the sea-level desert floor—it is the source of
storms, and, of course, life-giving water to the Cahuilla people of the region.

THE MOJAVE DESERT,
COACHELLA VALLEY
& COLORADO RIVER

THE COLORADO RIVER IS A PROVIDENT YEAR-ROUND LIFE-GIVER TO THE DESERT. EVEN when it wasn't dammed, its waters were reliable. Especially important are the broad flats and marshes of the lower river, caused by the narrows at Needles and Yuma. One of these special places is home to the **Mohave** (Hamákhava), who utilized a long stretch of river from Nevada to what is now Parker. This group of Hokan speakers were bordered on the south by another, the **Quechan** people. Both groups were unlike other California peoples: they had a strong tribal organization; they made wide use of pottery, a technique they seem to have borrowed from the early Hakataya culture to the east; and most unusual, they were and still are farmers.

The Colorado, much like the Nile, flooded once a year, covering the flatlands with a fertile layer of silt.

> ### THE COLORADO, MUCH LIKE THE NILE, FLOODED ONCE A YEAR, COVERING THE FLATLANDS WITH A FERTILE LAYER OF SILT.

Maize, beans, and several types of melons were then planted in this. Later, the Spanish arrival in Arizona in the 1600s brought the introduction of wheat, which the Colorado peoples adopted as a winter crop. The searing desert and barren mountains on both sides cannot support much large game, so fish, rabbits and other rodents and marsh birds were relied upon for meat.

Open brush shelters countered the intense summer sun, but winter homes were earth-covered dwellings made of saplings interspersed with mud. A replica of this *wattle & daub* construction has been erected on the grounds of the **Fort Yuma Reservation Museum.**

Between these two peoples, the **Chemehuevi** people settled in the Lake Havasu area. They are a branch of Southern Paiute who, in very early times, shared some farmland with the Mohave, though they were mainly desert dwellers. Their contemporary territory is in an area formerly occupied, but vacated over 150 years ago, by the Halchidhoma, who migrated eastward up the Gila River to live with the Maricopa. Transient residents on the lower Colorado of California were the **Cocopa**, now settled in Somerton, Arizona, and the **Yaqui**, who made forays into the Anza-Borrego area for game and water (hence, the place names of Yaqui Wells, Pass, Ridge, and Meadows).

The Native peoples of the Colorado have elected to develop their lands in various ways. Their populations did not escape the devastation and economic debasement of the Indian peoples during the past century; therefore, they are now finding ways to better themselves. Since the three largest of the reservations — the **Fort Mojave**, the **Fort Yuma,** and the immense **Colorado River Tribes** — have managed to keep most of their water rights through all the political shifts of the last century, they have been able to lease much of the fertile, arable land for a significant boost in their per capita incomes. The rocky, sloping **Chemehuevi Reservation** isn't arable, so the tribe is exploiting the white migration into the sunbelt by developing long-lease homesites on Lake Havasu, accompanied by a marina, res-

Desert Intaglios, Colorado River, honoring Yuman creation spirit

taurant, and other amenities, including a tribal craft shop and beach.

If you are interested in visiting large farms, try any of the Big 3 above (all straddle the state line). On the Colorado River Reservation you will find thousands of miles of canals, and at Fort Yuma, hydroponics for winter crops.

The **Colorado River Reservation** is distinctive in a number of ways. The people here are from four tribes: **Mohave, Chemehuevi, Navajo (Diné),** and **Hopi**. Members of the latter two tribes were brought here after World War II to work on some local projects. After the projects ended, the people remained; conditions here were better than back home.

All four tribes practice ceremonies particular to their respective cultures, and all participate jointly in National Indian Day festivities in September. A campground is available year-round, as is access to an excellent "working" museum, which sponsors various cultural classes and an excellent library. BIA and other governmental agencies have administration, health, and maintenance facilities here. The general feeling of this reservation is that of a progressive agricultural area.

Displayed on an alluvial bench above the Colorado River on the southwest end of the Reservation are the famous **Giant Desert Figures** of stylized animals and anthropomorphic figures, 95 to 167 feet long. It is believed that these symbols were "carved" or scooped from the desert surface (brown pebbles on a light-colored sand), honoring the ancient spirit of creation.

Fort Mojave Reservation tribal center is on the N side of Needles.

Chemehuevi Reservation is 15 mi. E of U.S. 95 on Lake Havasu Rd., 17 mi. S of Needles.

Colorado River Tribes Reservation is in California and Arizona; main facilities are in Parker, Arizona, on the road S from 95. Reservation maps at tribal headquarters.

Giant Desert Figures (Intaglios) are 15.3 mi. N of I-10 (Blythe) on U.S. 95.

Fort Yuma Reservation is the southeast corner of California, and is essentially a warm agricultural community. It's a fine place to be in January, if you don't like snow. The pueblo-like **Quechan Tribal Center**, a good tribal museum (1851), offices, and two venerable churches perch on a promontory overlooking the Colorado River and the reservation to the north and east. From this hill you may gaze out upon miles and miles of vegetables destined for the plates of America. Around the fields are at least two RV parks (camping, also) and high-stakes gaming halls. September Indian Days and March are powwow times.

Fort Yuma Reservation center is reached from I-80 via the Winterhaven Exit; turn east on the road going up the hill.

West of Fort Yuma and east of the Coachella Valley we encounter the Colorado River Desert dunes and the Chocolate Mountains, uninhabitable and among the world's driest regions. The Coachella Valley, however, has been host to Native peoples for many thousands of years. The evidence is there: two hundred feet above the sump of the Salton Sea, the shore of ancient Lake Cahuilla lines the edge of the mountains, and in the rocky "beaches" small depressions three to four feet in depth have been hollowed out. When the lake was full, some 10,000 years ago, fishermen would shoo fish into these little ponds and trap them. The lake dried up and the descendants of the fishermen remained — they are (in part) the Cahuilla people of today.

The **Cahuilla** are a people employing many ecological climates — from desert to temperate. Their desert rises, but this desert rises in places to over a mile in elevation, capturing enough rain and snow for extensive pine forests and green meadows. Their food included items such as cactus buds, corn, beans, and melons from the lowlands, to piñon, acorns, berries, seeds, mountain sheep, and deer from the uplands. Towering

Top Left: Amidst the booming agricultural spread of vegetables, a Ft. Yuma resident maintains a secluded, shady home.

Bottom Left: Spectacular Palm Canyon on the Agua Caliente Reservation at Palm Springs, is one of only a few such water sources and ecological preserves in the southern desert area. The tribe takes great pride in careful management of this and the other palm canyons on the reservation.

Top Right: Many years ago, the Indian Agency used these buildings to supervise activities on the Torres-Martinez Reservation. They are now designated an National Landmark. Today the tribes manages its own affairs in a small building nearby.

Bottom Right: An arroyo of the Soboba Reservation carries meagre runoff from the lower, drier foothills of the San Jacinto Mountains. Stream beds like these nourish trees, shrubs, and grasses on much southern California Indian land.

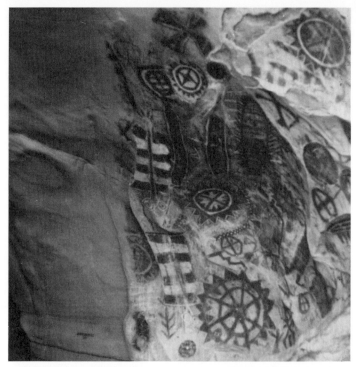

Top Left: Remarkably well preserved and of priceless value, these girls' hand prints were used in puberty ceremonies by ancient dwellers near a spring in the desert region near Perris (Riverside Co.).

Top Right: The Chumash Painted Cave bears one of the most remarkable examples of ancient Indian rock art in North America. Some of the designs are thought to honor the spirits of Sun and Moon; others are undeciphered.

Bottom Left and Right: Near the Ft. Mojave Reservation at the Needles narrows of the Colorado River, is this ancient, intricate labyrinthine maze of shallow ditches. As the spirits of the dead travel downriver past the Needles, evil spirits attempting to follow them are entrapped and become lost in the labyrinth. Mohave people continue to hold ceremonies at this site, though it is partially defaced by a pipeline and a freeway.

over all is the 10,800-ft. San Jacinto Peak and behind it to the west, the immense granite pylon Tahquitz (tá-kwish), the Cahuilla earth center. Tahquitz — the source of storms and lightning and rain, which are evidence of the power of the spirits.

The Cahuilla and their neighbors to the west, the **Kamia** and **Ipai-Tipai**, originally won by treaty a very large bloc in Imperial, San Diego, and Riverside Counties. Before long, the usual axing away of Indian land occurred, and today's land is but a small fraction. Nevertheless, their southern California Indian country is fairly ample — the Cahuilla own some ten reservations including two that are shared. Most of this land is undeveloped or sparsely settled, as in the Cahuilla and Los Coyotes Reservations, making the land a practically pristine example of ecological preservation. (See p. 49.)

The shapes of the Torres-Martinez, Soboba, **Morongo**, and **Agua Caliente** Reservations were the bizarre result of government land policies — land "awarded" in a checkerboard of alternate square miles. The accidental flooding of nearly half of the Torres-Martinez in 1905 did not result in a compensatory grant of land; however, only a few persons live on the many remaining flat, deserty acres, although a large number of acres are leased to agricultural enterprises. Their people are housed in new homes against the Santa Rosa Mountains front.

Several reservations are making other enterprises pay. The **Cabazon** is right on I-5 in Indio, and one of its members is the originator of California Indian high-stakes bingo. The Morongo, up the road, also sports a bingo palace, as does Soboba, over the mountain. The largest Native enterprise in the area, though, is Palm Springs. Half the city is Indian land leased by the **Agua Caliente** tribe, which owns every other square-mile section. The tribe also jealously preserves the **Palm Canyons**, the source of their cul-

ture and a unique ecological niche.

To gain an appreciation of the Indianness of the Cahuilla culture, a visit to the **Morongo Reservation** and the small, informative **Malki Museum** is imperative. The Morongo is in a beautiful, peaceful setting.

The Cahuilla section of the **Palm Springs Desert Museum** is informatively presented, and the Agua Caliente tribe itself is readying plans for a culture center of its own. Additionally, the **Palm Canyon Trading Post** serves as a book and crafts shop and trailhead for a tour of the Canyon. The Agua Caliente Tribe sponsors an Indian Market in March.

Morongo Reservation tribal offices are at the Potrero Rd. Exit off I-10; for the Malki Museum take the Field Rd. Exit, both E of Banning.

Palm Canyon Trading Post is at the extreme S end of Palm Canyon Dr. in Palm Springs.

Beyond the cities and highways and bordering the desert, **Los Coyotes**, an ancient Cahuilla land, invites one to visit. The camping facilities are primitive, but the vistas of Mt. Palomar and the desert are superb in this nearly unspoiled Indian country. The **Cupeño** are a small group whose language is a variety of Cahuilla. They once lived in a few villages grouped around the Warner Springs adjacent to what is now the Los Coyotes. Greedy whites demanded ownership of the springs and forced the removal of the Cupeño to the Pala Reservation. Cupa Days is still celebrated the first weekend in May at Pala.

The people of the lower Mojave Desert and San Bernardino Mountains just to the north of the Cahuilla were small groups of **Serrano** and **Vanyume**. Much the same can be said of their desert and mountain mode of life that was said of the Cahuilla. The Vanyume were totally dispersed before 1900; the **San Manuel Reservation** is the present-day home of the Serrano, with a magnificent bingo palace that finally provides a comfortable income for the people.

San Manuel is at the N end of Victoria Ave. in Highland (San Bernardino).

SOUTHWESTERN CALIFORNIA AND THE SOUTHERN COAST

BIG SUR TO SAN DIEGO

LANGUAGE KEY

Hokan

Uto-Aztecan

Esselen

VENTANA PEAKS

Salinan

SAN LUIS OBISPO

Chumash

SANTA BARBARA

Fernandeño/Gabrielino

LOS ANGELES

Juaneño/
Luiseño

Salton
Sea

MT. PALOMAR

Ipai

MT. LAGUNA

Tipai (Kamia)

SAN DIEGO

Dashed line: No defined territorial limits

THE PEOPLES	THE RESERVATIONS AND ORGANIZATIONS	

Hokan Speakers [b]
Esselen, Salinan, Chumash, Kumeyaay (Kamia), Tipai, or Ipai, (the latter three formerly called Diegueño)

Santa Ynez, Campo, Manzanita, LaPosta, Cuyapaipe, Sycuan, Viejas, Barona, Capitan Grande, Inaja-Cosmit, Santa Ysabel, Mesa Grande, San Pascual, Pala* Reservations, Jamul Village, Window To The West (Esselen private land);
organizations: Carmel Mission Indians, Coastal Band of Chumash, Ventureño Chumash, Candelaria American Indian Council, Salinan Tribe

[b] *Hokan is an ancient language group found in diverse areas of the state, and is distantly related to groups of northern and central Mexico.*

Uto-Aztecan Speakers [e]
Takic: Gabrielino-Fernadeño, Luiseño-Juaneño

Pala*, Mission Reserve, Rincon, La Jolla, Pauma-Yuima, Pechanga, Soboba* Reservations; dedicated land: Satwiwa (in Santa Monica Mountains NRA); *organizations*: Juaneño Band of Mission Indians, Atahun Shoshones of San Juan Capistrano, San Luis Rey Band of Mission Indians

[e] *Shoshonean is one of a large family of Uto-Aztecan languages spoken in the Great Basin, in eastern and southern California, by the Comanches, and by the Aztecs of Mexico. (See also p. 111.)*

* Shared with other groups.

▲ *Tom Little Bear Nason, a leader of the Esselen tribe, shows us grinding rocks of his people in Carmel Valley.*

SOUTHWESTERN CALIFORNIA & THE SOUTHERN COAST BIG SUR TO SAN DIEGO

THE SOUTHERN COASTAL HOKAN LAND COVERED A LARGE AMOUNT OF TERRITORY, BUT THESE WERE among the least populous peoples of the area. Their lands are mountainous and not as fertile as those of the Shoshonean peoples of the Los Angeles Basin.

Immediately to the south of the Costanoan peoples of Monterey Bay are **Esselen** lands, twelve hundred acres of which have been assiduously preserved in (private) Indian hands since the Mission era. Though the tribal character has been severely diminished, family members still own the lands and hold occasional gatherings. The tribe has formed a corporation, **Window To The West**, whose many activities foster the renewed interest in this and other Native American cultures and enable outsiders to experience the wilderness of Big Sur.

Early life of this people is poorly documented, though it must not have differed much from that of the Costanoan and Miwok coastal peoples to the north or the Chumash to the south.

Pa-che-pus (Esselen ranch) is found 2 mi. S of Jamesburg on Tassajara Rd., some 10 mi. SE of Carmel Valley. Inaccessible in wet weather.

In an especially poignant demonstration of the failure of missions, the **Salinan** people were practically wiped out when gathered into no less than *three* missions — Soledad, San Antonio, and San Miguel. By 1834 the missions themselves were left with hardly a congregation whatsoever; there are few towns within many miles. Soledad is in ruins; the other two rely on outsiders to maintain the church. But... a small nucleus of Salinan families who eke out a living in the Coast Range Mountains and Big Sur have recently begun to organize in the neighborhood of the San Antonio Mission. The California renaissance continues.

> SOUTH OF MONTEREY BAY, 1200 ACRES OF ESSELEN LANDS HAVE BEEN PRESERVED IN PRIVATE INDIAN HANDS SINCE THE MISSION ERA.

The **Chumash** inhabited the coastal and mountain land further to the south, between San Luis Obispo and Thousand Oaks, as well as the westernmost offshore islands. Their land was varied, and their culture was rich in industry. They built 25-foot, decorated plank boats, *tomols*, to ferry persons and materials to their steatite (soapstone) mines on the offshore islands and to fish from; they harvested asphalt from the oily oozes on the Santa Barbara coast for use as glue and sealants; they fashioned steatite into fireproof stoneware, in place of pottery; they built huge hemispherical houses of reed some 50 feet in diameter; they produced beautiful finely-coiled baskets and carved wooden bowls; and they executed the most fantastic rock paintings ever seen.

Although meanings were similar to those of other Hokan groups, the forms of Chumash religion were unusual: the main deity was Shup (Chi-ngich-ngish of the Luiseño), occasionally represented by a feathered symbol hung in the large reed homes or in the center of a brush-enclosed ceremonial circle. Shark was honored, especially by those near the sea; Sun and Moon were honored, and

Four Directions & Cosmic Sun Chumash Painted Cave, Santa Barbara Co. (See also photo on page 116

shamans painted fantastic ceremonial circles and wheels, it is said, while in a trance state in part induced by toloache. The great wheels are exceptionally symbolic renderings of a cosmos inclusive of sun, moon, and stars, executed with uncommon artistic perception.

Chumash villages also built sweathouses, as did almost all California groups. One other characteristic shared with other California peoples was the sanctioning of berdache (transvestites), men who preferred the customs, habits, and company of women.

After the white invasion, the Chumash fared somewhat better than their northern neighbors, perhaps owing to an ability to integrate their industry into the variety of economic pursuits offered by the white population. Even so, they were given only a tiny fragment of land, the **Santa Ynez Reservation,** as their own, under the direct supervision of the church at Santa Ynez. A recent article in *U.S. News and World Report* reported that the Chumash had long ago become extinct, but that is news to the several Chumash organizations that preserve the Chumash culture and activities.

Common to the Chumash and the Gabrielinos is **Satwiwa**, a scenic undeveloped area in the western part of the Santa Monica Mountains National Recreation Area, set aside specifically for interpretive use by and for Native American peoples. Go there. The hawks will soar above you; the grasses and flowers will scent the air. Know that this is Indian country.

Santa Ynez Reservation is at Santa Ynez, E of Solvang, on State Hwy. 246.

Satwiwa, part of Santa Monica Mountains N.R.A., is reached from U.S. 101 Wendy Dr. Exit (W of Thousand Oaks), W on Potrero Rd. to Rancho Sierra Vista and Satwiwa.

> THE HAWKS WILL SOAR ABOVE YOU; THE GRASSES AND FLOWERS WILL SCENT THE AIR. KNOW THAT THIS IS INDIAN COUNTRY.

Under the southern arc of the Coast Range mountains of Ventura/Los Angeles/Kern Counties lie the ancestral lands of the **Kitanemuk** and **Tataviam** peoples, both very small groups who were totally removed by Army sweeps in the 1850s. It is believed that none of their descendants remain today.

The coastal shelf which contains San Fernando and Los Angeles, extending through Orange County to San Diego was the most highly missionized portion of the state. Few of the padres who controlled this region were sufficiently interested in the Indian language or culture to record much. They were more interested in preserving souls than customs. Most early language and tribal customs were obliterated. A notable exception can be found in some closely guarded rituals of the Luiseños, well-hidden from the Padres, and extant to this day. Even the peoples' name for themselves is uncertain, so ethnologists use the name of the nearest mission: **Gabrielino** (San Gabriel), **Fernandeño** (San Fernando), **Luiseño** (San Luis Rey), **Juaneño** (San Juan Capistrano), **Diegueño** (San Diego). The first two and the third and fourth are usually grouped together, as their customs seem similar. The identity of the Diegueño is better known, and have been given differing names by ethnologists: **Ipai** for those living east of La Jolla, **Tipai** for the people of the San Diego area, and **Kamia** (Kumeyaay) for those further east up to the Anza-Borrego desert. **Kumeyaay**, however, is the contemporary term preferred by all three.

Life among the **Gabrielino/ Fernandeño** peoples probably did not differ much from that of the Chumash, for their land and biotic zones presented similar environments. Since the culture

▶ *This lofty and elegant building on the Santa Ynéz Reservation houses their community center.*

▶ *One of the few extant revered Gabrielino sites in the Los Angeles area is Eagle Rock, preserved from the freeway by the California Highway Department, but defaced by aerial intrusions. A powwow drum organization honors the place with occasional dances across the highway.*

has been so decimated, archaeological investigation is probably the only means of making a comparison. Among these groups, dwellings and articles of village life also seem to have been similar. As with the majority of southerly California peoples, they were skilled at sand painting; they held puberty ceremonies for both men and women; and in trading they used a form of counting by knots in a string, like the quipú of the Incas.

A hiding place need not be in the remote fastness of a forest; it can be the vastness of a spread-out city. For many decades, the Gabrielino families kept their heritage quiet, their relationships known only to themselves and to a few others. They had no land base at all. Within the last decade, they have found that organizing can yield numerous benefits and pride in being Native American. Today the tribe (in several groupings) estimates that 1800 persons are direct descendants of the Natives of the Mission era. One group, known as the Tóngva, holds regular meetings. Another instance of the revival of the California Indian presence is revealed.

One revered Gabrielino site is the eagle to be found at **Eagle Rock**, preserved by the highway department on Highway 134.

The **Luiseño/Juaneño** groups to the south were distinctly different from the Gabrielino to the north or the Cahuilla to their east. Of note were their sand paintings, of elaborate symbology, some of which have been published. Their territory extended from the coast to Mt. Palomar; they have retained reservation land on the sites of older villages and some undeveloped land. Early on, the missions did allow some members to live within their villages, a situation which contributed to less cultural destruction than with those forced to live in the compounds. Today, Indian life on reservations such as **Pala**, **La Jolla** (not the coastal city), **Rincon**, and **Pechanga** is reminiscent of a time past — quiet, steady, and remarkably preserving some

of the oldest rituals and ceremonies (usually quite private). The fiestas, normally on saints' days, are the major occasions for gatherings of the people.

Pala Reservation is a particularly pleasant place to visit. A full-service tribal campground invites us to stay and learn; the interior walls of the Pala Mission church are adorned with strange paintings of faces; and the burial ground retains an ancient custom of placing personal goods on the graves. La Jolla, (Sp., *the jewel*) lying along the slopes of Mt. Palomar, is a most inviting place. A shady riverside campground is one place to stay, while the old village with its mountainside church and a very modern water park (slides and pools) entice us to linger. Soboba and Rincon also entice visitors with bingo. Some Luiseños and Juaneños of this region who never had a land base have recently organized for tribal recognition.

Pala Reservation village is at Hwy. S-16 and State Hwy. 76, 25 mi. E of Oceanside.

La Jolla Reservation is 2 mi. E of Palomar exit on State Hwy. 76.

Rincon Reservation is on County Rd. S-6, 10 mi. NE of Escondido.

Pechanga Reservation is at Pechanga Rd. (47,000 block) of County Rd. S-16 just S of the intersection with State Hwy. 79 (Rancho California).

The southwest of California is the territory of the **Kumeyaay** (formerly called **Diegueño**) a group of rather independent bands speaking Hokan-based dialects. Their lands extend from the coast to the cool-in-summer highlands of the southern Coast Range, and eastward to the desert. The coastal country and the Salton Sea margins are some of the oldest known Indian-inhabited parts of the United States; some middens (garbage piles) date back 20,000 years, though more settled occupation took place only 7,000 years ago.

The peoples of this region were rather dispersed, not building great structures as did their northern neighbors. Apparently, small mat- or thatch-covered brush shelters, or caves served for dwellings. These peoples were sophisticated dry-land farmers, employing unique erosion control diversion dams, having adapted some techniques from their Quechan cousins. They also traded widely, from the Pacific coast to the Colorado River. Trade included acorns from the oak-studded highlands and skilfully woven baskets. Their religion centered about a spiritual guardian who takes on an animal form. As usual, Coyote was distrusted, while Eagle and Mountain Lion were revered. Toloache (datura) came late, 1800s, and pottery somewhat earlier, from the Quechan.

Today, these peoples live in some twelve reservations, most of which are very lightly populated, though some are developing their assets. **Viejas**, for instance, has a comfortable RV Park and campground, just off I-8, as well as gaming operations. **Barona** has a bingo hall, though a visit to this green upland valley and the quaint mission church is pleasant in itself. The **Campo Reservation** has neither bingo nor campground, but visiting this remote place, with undeveloped scenery is rewarding to the senses. It is a place bearing evident history and solitude with its old clapboard church and environmentally-oriented tribal hall almost invisible on the chapparal hillside. Ancient oaks shade the valleys; coyotes sing at night. Some Campo Kamia residents possess the unusual right of dual citizenship with Mexico, since traditional tribal territories extend some distance into Baja California Norte.

With less solitude, but possessing an evident history, is the **Sycuan Reservation**, its high hill topped by ancient and modern churches and an attractive tribal hall. (The bingo operation is fortunately tucked into a valley.)

An excellent unifying presentation of the history and environments of these several southern California peoples is to be found at the **San Diego Museum of Man** in Balboa Park.

Viejas Reservation lies on the N side of I-8 at E. Willows Rd. Exit (near Alpine).

▲ *The rugged terrain of the Ventana Wilderness is the ancestral home of the Esselen people.*

Barona Reservation is somewhat remote, on Wildcat Cyn. Rd., just NE of Lakeside or S of Ramona.

Campo Reservation is on I-8 at Live Oak Spgs., but take Olde Hwy 80 1/4 mi. to gravel road S to State Hwy. 94. (I-8 passes by two other reservations at this exit, both nearly unpopulated, yet excellent examples of ecologically pristine lands.)

Sycuan Reservation is E of El Cajon off I-8, Alpine-Tavern Exit, S on Tavern Rd. to Dehesa Rd., 3 mi. to Dehesa Fire Dept. and Sycuan.

Reacting to increasing pressures from the white community to relieve the shameful situation of the Native Americans, Congress in 1891 established Sherman Institute, under the auspices of the Indian Service (later the Bureau of Indian Affairs). Sherman was to be a boarding school for the "relief of the Mission Indians"; augmented by a hospital in 1902, now a clinic. For a time in the 1930s and 40s, California persuaded the BIA to exclude California residents, preferring that state schools educate the Indian population. This ineffective and hypocritical policy was reversed recently, and the **Sherman Indian High School**, as it is now known, was modernized and expanded. The school offers a comprehensive, accredited high school curriculum for 600 students, with a specific emphasis on Native American culture. A museum on the campus highlights important events in the school's history, as well as Native American history.

Sherman Indian High School is located at 9010 Magnolia Ave, Riverside. A pass to visit within the campus is obtainable at the gate. The museum is open to the public.

▲ *Bottom Left: Viejas Res. (Kumeyaay) occupies a high, cool, chaparral and oak valley of the San Diego Co. Coast Range.*

◄ *Top Left: Summer haze hangs over the mountains of the Sycuan Reservation (Kamia), in San Diego Co. This land is most tranquil, other areas are more active with bingo and fire department calls.*

► *Right Page: A simple, graceful clapboard chapels on the tiny Jamul Indian Village.*

LATTER-DAY MIGRATIONS INTO CALIFORNIA

THE MAGNET THAT IS CALIFORNIA HAS ATTRACTED PEOPLE OF ALL RACES, AND Native Americans are no exception. As early as the 1930s, the Depression encouraged the migration of Indian people from parts of the U.S. hit by drought and unemployment. World War II drew Indian workers to California's shipyards, agricultural fields, and urban-based industries. These peoples came from Indian and Aleut Alaska, from Oklahoma and the Dakotas and the upper Midwest, from Arizona and New Mexico, from the Native peoples of Hawaii, and from as far as New York. These new arrivals brought with them their tribal customs and yearnings for their rituals and ceremonies.

Consequently, the centers where these peoples settled became nuclei for the organization of powwow societies and drums. (A *drum* is not just the actual large, horizontal "bass" drum, but the society of singers and drummers as well.) The drums are based on the music and rituals of Plains, Great Basin, and some Southwest and Southeast tribes. Their style is frequently called Intertribal or "Pan-Indian," reflecting an amalgam of different customs.

At powwows we are presented with the costumes and dancing styles of many different peoples from all over the U.S. Commonly at powwows, very special songs and dancing may be invited, such as Pueblo White Eagle, Cherokee Corn Dance, Hoop dances, or Navajo (Diné) clan dances. Even displaced Iroquois (originally from New York) have organized in Long Beach as the Iroquois Social Dancers (traditional storytelling and dancing). Not found at powwows, Hawaiian Native peoples dance at their own annual festivals in the San Francisco and Los Angeles areas. One finds a very large number of the Native people from other states engaged in advocate groups, endeavoring to better their people at "home" and in the cities, in all areas from health to housing to employment.

Hollywood's film industry has drawn a number of very able Native American actors since the 1920s. As all must know, the portrayals of Indians in the earlier days, however, were stylized and stilted and erroneous, hardly resembling any tribe seen before or since. In the 1990s, Indian actors still find employment in film, and finally, parts are taking on much more realism.

California's agricultural fields and employment opportunities attracted thousands, if not millions of Natives, often transient, from Mexican, Central, and South American homelands. If there are tribal rituals for the people of Yaqui, Aztec, Zapotec, Maya, and other Native origins, they are to be found only at home, not in the barrios and *bracero* camps of California, with some important exceptions. In Sacramento, San Francisco, Los Angeles, Orange County, and San Diego groups of Aztec Dancers (Nahuatl speakers) have organized to dance.

They will tell you that they dance because they must; and so it seems. On certain feast days, they gather and dance all day; spectators are invited, but these are not public events. (See Calendar, Appendix A, Festivals.)

APPENDICES

A CALENDAR
OF CALIFORNIA'S NATIVE AMERICAN EVENTS
APPENDIX A

These events are open to the general public, Most functions: NO CAMERAS OR ALCOHOL. Certain events are held on fixed dates, others are held on specific weekends or approximate dates, which may vary. For further information, please call first or contact your local American Indian Center.

WINTER

MID-JANUARY
Southwest Museum, Pasadena
Los Angeles Native American Film Festival (213) 221-2164

FEBRUARY 19th & 27th
San Francisco Honoring the Longest Walk (19th);
Recognition of Wounded Knee Occupation (27th).
Intl. Indian Treaty Council (415) 566-0251

FEBRUARY 21st
& LAST WEEKEND IN FEB.
Los Angeles, Olvera St./Lincoln Park
Cuauhtémoc Day: Mexican Indian dances, entertainment.
Xipe Totec, Templo Flor, participants (714) 774-9803,
(213) 664-6433

San Francisco (location varies)
Cuauhtémoc Day: Mexican Indian dances. Xitlalli,
participant (415) 586-0435

SPRING

LATE FEBRUARY/MARCH
Santa Rosa Rancheria, Lemoore, Kings Co.
Spiritual Renewal: All tribes dances and songs (all night)
(209) 924-1278

WEEKEND IN MARCH NEAREST EQUINOX (21st)
Pasadena, La Villa Park
Fiesta de Primavera: Mexican tribal dances, food.
Xipe Totec (714) 774-9803

Sacramento (location varies)
Spring Fiesta: Mexican tribal dances, food. Quetzalcoatl/Xitlalli
(916) 739-1105

LATE MARCH WEEKEND
Agua Caliente Reservation, Palm Springs
Palm Springs Indian Market and Tribal Festival (619) 325-5673

PRE-EASTER
Pala Reservation, N San Diego Co.
Holy Week services in Mission Chapel (619) 742-3784

EASTER
Quartz Valley Rancheria, Siskiyou Co.
Wintun Easter gathering: Indian card games, music, pot luck
(916) 468-2468

1ST WEEK IN APRIL
California State University, Sacramento
Native American Culture Week (916) 278-6595

4th WEEKEND IN APRIL
Kule Loklo, Point Reyes Natl. Seashore, Marin Co.
Strawberry Festival: songs, dances, prayers (415) 663-1092

1st WEEKEND IN MAY
Pala Reservation, N San Diego Co.
Cupa Days: invited dances (619) 742-3784

Redding, Caldwell Park
Big Time: drums, singers, crafts.
Sponsor: Redding Museum & Cultural Center (916) 225-4050

San Juan Bautista, San Benito Co.
American Indian & Western Artists Show:
tribal arts and culture, drums, dancers, singers, food.
Reyna's Gallerias (408) 623-2379

WEEKEND NEAR MAY 5th
Berkeley, Martin Luther King Park
Cinco de Mayo: invited Mexican dances, food, entertainment.
Xitlalli, participant (415) 586-0435

MID-MAY
Anderson Marsh State Park, Lake Co.
Native American Cultural Day: food, craft instruction, dances
(707) 847-3397

State Indian Museum, Sacramento
Honored Elders Day: food, invited dances, songs, storytelling
(916) 324-0971

Upper Kern River, Sequoia Natl. Forest, above Kernville
Monache Gathering: tribal & intertribal drums and dancing,
elders talks, sweat lodge, Bear Dance
(619) 376-4240 or 878-2523

3rd WEEKEND IN MAY
Jesse Peter Native American Art Museum, Santa Rosa Jr.
College. Day Under the Oaks: crafts, food, tribal dancers,
storytelling, children's activities (707) 527-4479

MEMORIAL DAY WEEKEND
Folsom, Pacific Western Traders Spring Art Show & Indian
Market: food, dances (916) 985-3851

Morongo Reservation, Banning, Riverside Co.
Malki Museum Fiesta & Powwow: So. Cal. tribal dances, bird
songs, food (714) 849-7289

Sierra Mono Museum, North Fork, Madera Co.
Memorial Day Gathering: honoring of the elders (209) 877-2115

1st WEEKEND IN JUNE
Ya-ka-ama, Forestville, Sonoma Co.
Spring Fair: dances, crafts, food, games, sports (707) 887-1541

1st WEEK IN JUNE
San Diego Museum of Man, San Diego
Indian Fair Days: dancing, crafts (619) 274-0313

1st SUNDAY IN JUNE
Pala Reservation, N. San Diego Co.
Corpus Christi: religious festival (619) 742-3784

1st or 2nd SATURDAY IN JUNE
Marin Museum of the Am. Indian, Novato, Marin Co.
Indian Trade Festival (415) 897-4064

San Juan Bautista, San Benito Co.
Honoring of the Elders Powwow: traditional dances, run, benefit
(408) 726-3320 or 728-8471

2nd WEEK IN JUNE
Satwiwa, Santa Monica Mountains Natl. Recreation Area,
Gabrielino & Chumash gathering and powwow (818) 597-9192

A CALENDAR OF CALIFORNIA'S
NATIVE AMERICAN EVENTS, continued

SUMMER

MID-JUNE, NEAR SOLSTICE
San Francisco or **Sacramento** (location varies),
Fiesta de Maiz (Corn Festival): Mexican ceremonies and dances.
Xitlalli (415) 586-0435 or (916) 739-1105

3rd WEEKEND IN JUNE
Visitors Center, Yosemite Nat'l Park
Indian Day Big Time: Miwok dances, sweats, big dinner,
handgames. Park info (209) 372-4461, or card to: J. Johnson,
Y.N.P. 95389 (Adm. fee to Park; Nat. Ams. free; camping)

JULY 4th WEEKEND
Hoopa Reservation, Humboldt Co.
Hoopa Rodeo, ceremonial dances (916) 625-4110

Hopland Rancheria, Hopland, S Mendocino Co.
Annual picnic: dances, food (707) 744-1647

Santa Ynez Reservation, Santa Barbara Co.
July 4th Powwow: crafts, food, Chumash and other dances (805)
688-7997

Stewarts Point Rancheria (Kashaya), W Sonoma Co.
Tribal dances, potluck on July 4th (707) 785-2594

2nd WEEKEND IN JULY
Lava Beds Natl. Monument, Captain Jack's Stronghold, Modoc Co.
Modoc Gathering: ceremonies, dances, songs, live crafts
(916) 667-2282

Wassama Roundhouse State Park, Ahwahnee, Madera Co.
Gathering Day (Yokuts & others): dances, demonstrations, arts
& crafts, sweat lodge, BBQ (209) 833-2332

3rd WEEKEND IN JULY
Kule Loklo, Point Reyes Natl. Seashore, Marin Co.
Big Time Celebration (Miwok, Pomo, Wappo, others): trade
booths, native foods, demonstrations (415) 663-1092

Mission Plaza, San Luis Obispo
American Indian Art Festival: juried art, drums, crafts, food.
Host: Chumash tribe. Sponsor: Reyna's Gallerias (408) 623-2379

LAST WEEKEND IN JULY
Ukiah, City Park, Todd Grove
Native American Day: several Pomo and other dancers, booths,
arts & crafts, salmon feed, demonstrations (707) 468-1180

1st WEEKEND IN AUGUST
Sierra Mono Museum, Northfork, Madera Co.
Indian Fair: dances, food, games, crafts, sports (209) 877-2115

Smith River at Ne-lo-chun-don (S. Bank Rd.), Del Norte Co.
Naydosh (Ten Night Dance): pot luck Fri. & Sat. nights.
Sponsor: Tolowa Nation (707) 464-7332

3rd WEEKEND IN AUGUST
Fort Ross State Historic Park, Sonoma Co.
Indian Day: Coastal Indian dances, displays, arts & crafts

LAST WEEKEND IN AUGUST
Santa Rosa Rancheria, Lemoore, Kings Co.
Santa Rosa Days: dancing (tribal & C/W), food, baseball tourney
(209) 924-1278

LATE AUGUST or SEPTEMBER
Hoopa Reservation, Humboldt Co.
White Deerskin and Jumping Dances (biennial) (916) 625-4211

AUTUMN

LABOR DAY, 1st MONDAY IN SEPTEMBER

Bishop Reservation, N Inyo Co.
Labor Day Celebration: handgames, sports, picnic
(619) 873-3584

SATURDAY AFTER LABOR DAY

Tuolumne Rancheria, Tuolumne Co.
Acorn Festival: dances, food. (209) 928-4277

1st WEEKEND IN SEPTEMBER

San Juan Bautista, Hollister, San Benito Co.
Fall Indian Fair: crafts, juried art, exhibition dances. Reyna's
Gallerias: (408) 623-2379

2nd WEEKEND IN SEPTEMBER

San Jose, Prusch Farm Park
Indian Summer Festival: dances crafts, food, fun run, shows.
Sponsor: Indian Center of San Jose (408) 971-9622

3rd WEEKEND IN SEPTEMBER

Pala Reservation, N San Diego Co.
Fiesta-Pala Fire Dept. benefit: crafts, food, social dancing, softball
(619) 742-1632

Riverside, W. Riverside Co.
Riverside Indian Days

CALIFORNIA INDIAN DAYS 4th WEEKEND IN SEPTEMBER

Barona Reservation, Lakeside, San Diego Co.
Indian Days observance. (619) 281-5964

California State Indian Museum
Sacramento California Indian Days: dances, crafts, food
(Location may vary.) (916) 445-4209 or 324-0971

Chaw-Se Indian Grinding Rocks State Park,
Pine Grove, Amador Co.
Big Time: dances, games, crafts, food (209) 296-7488

Colorado River Reservation, Parker, AZ
Combined Colorado River Tribes Fair & Indian Days: pageant,
powwow, food, games, dances (602) 669-9211

Crescent City (beachfront), Del Norte Co.
California Indian Day: salmon bake, dances, arts & crafts, stick
games. Sponsor: Tolowa Nation (707) 464-7332

Ft. Yuma Reservation, SE Imperial Co.
Indian Days: powwow, food (619) 572-0213

Porterville, Fairgrounds, Tulare Co.
Native American Heritage Celebration: powwow, Indian arts,
stories. Nat. Am. Heritage Committee (209) 784-4509

Rancho Los Alamitos, Long Beach
Gabrielino Gathering of the People, *Puvugna*: dances, exhibits,
activities, stories (213) 431-3541

Roseville (environs)
California Indian Days: Powwow, crafts, food, camping
(916) 920-0285

Round Valley Reservation, Covelo, Mendocino Co.
Indian Days: crafts, food, intertribal and Calif. dances camping,
handgames (707) 983-6126

San Diego, Balboa Park (6th & Laurel)
American Indian Day: dancing, arts & crafts, education, health
clinic, food (619) 234-2158

Ya-ka-ama, Forestville, Sonoma Co.
Indian Summer Harvest Festival: arts & crafts, dances, garden
harvest, elders dinner (707) 887-1541

A CALENDAR OF CALIFORNIA'S
NATIVE AMERICAN EVENTS, continued

AUTUMN

EARLY OCTOBER
Quincy (several locations)
Northern Sierra Indian Days: powwow, arts & crafts, film festival (adm.) (916) 283-3402

2nd SATURDAY IN OCTOBER
California State Indian Museum,
Sacramento Acorn Day: history, dances, acorn eats (916) 445-0071

2nd WEEKEND IN OCTOBER
Ft. Mojave Reservation, Needles, E San Bernardino Co.
Annual Powwow: crafts, food, parade, gourd dances, bird songs, intertribal drums (619) 326-4591

OCTOBER 12th
Sacramento (location varies)
Fiesta de Los Guerreros Aguilas y Jaguares: Aztec ceremony of transition from boyhood to manhood. Sponsor: Quetzalcoatl/Xitlalli (916) 739-1105

San Francisco (location varies)
International Day of Solidarity; Intl. Indian Treaty Council (415) 566-0251

MID-OCTOBER
Yurok Reservation, Humboldt Co.
Yurok dances (biennial) (916) 625-4275

Pala Reservation, N San Diego Co.
Children's Festival of St. Francis of Assisi (619) 742-3784

3rd WEEKEND IN OCTOBER
Henry Cowell Redwoods State Park, Santa Cruz Co.
Ohlone Day: participation in many "old ways," making baskets, arrowheads, games, food (adm. to park) (408) 335-3174

4th WEEKEND IN OCTOBER
Kule Loklo, Point Reyes Natl. Seashore, Marin Co.
Acorn Festival: songs, dances, prayers of thanksgiving for the acorn crop (415) 663-1092

NOVEMBER 1-2:
DIA DE LOS MUERTOS
Los Angeles, Echo Park area
Songs, prayers, esp. Sp. language tribes.
Sponsor: Templo Flor (213) 664-6433

Sacramento (location varies)
Vigil, prayers, Mexican ceremonial dances. Sponsor: Xitlalli (916) 739-1105

San Francisco, Mission neighborhood, Velación (late night).
Sponsors: Xitlalli, Instituto Familiár de La Raza (415) 586-0435

Campo Reservation, SE San Diego Co.
All Saints Day Festival: Mass for the Departed (619) 478-5251

EARLY NOVEMBER
San Francisco, Palace of Fine Arts
American Indian Film Festival: films on Native American subjects, crafts, food (adm.) (415) Call information.

1st WEEKEND IN NOVEMBER
(Biennial, even years)
Redding Museum and Arts Center
Redding Indian Heritage Days: dances honoring Wintu, Pit River peoples, food, demonstrations, oral tradition (916) 225-4155

2nd WEEKEND IN NOVEMBER
Eureka, Redwood Acres, Humboldt Co.
Intertribal Thanksgiving for Honoring Elders: powwow, arts & crafts, potlatch for elders. Coord.: Pete Taylor (707) 455-8451

NOVEMBER 15th
Santa Ysabel Mission, central San Diego Co.
Feast Day at the Mission church

LATE NOVEMBER WEEKEND
California State Indian Museum, Sacramento
Native American Film Festival: Films and live dances (916) 445-0971

THANKSGIVING DAY
Alcatraz Island, San Francisco
Sunrise ceremony honoring sun dancers and thanksgiving prayers. Intl. Ind. Treaty Council (415) 566-0251

DECEMBER 12th:
FIESTA OF OUR LADY OF GUADALUPE
San Diego (location varies)
Sponsor: Danza Mexicayotl (619) 428-1115

Los Angeles, Loreto Church, Echo Park
Ceremonies, dances, food. Xipe Totec, participant
(714) 774-9803

WINTER

MID-DECEMBER
Folsom, Pacific Western Traders
Annual Christmas Show: fine Indian arts & crafts
(916) 985-3851

Sacramento (location varies)
Fiesta de Tonanacin (Mother Earth Festival). Sponsor, with others: Xitlalli (916) 739-1105

DECEMBER 21st
SOLSTICE
Smith River at Ne-lo-chun-don (S. Bank Rd.), Del Norte Co.
Indian New Year: dances and celebration. Sponsor: Tolowa Nation (707) 464-7332

Pa-che-pus (Esselen Ranch), Monterey Co.
Solstice Celebration: potluck and dances (408) 659-2153

DECEMBER 25th
Christmas services at all reservation churches.

POWWOWS

Note: Powwows are primarily, but not exclusively, intertribal dances, ceremonies, or festivals of Native American peoples from other states, who reside in California, and who wish to maintain their tribal traditions, though many miles from home.

COLLEGES, SCHOOLS AND OTHER SPONSORS

MARCH
Stockton, San Joaquin Delta Coll. (209) 474-5151

Turlock, Stanislaus Coll.

D-Q U with Univ. of California, Davis (916) 752-1001

APRIL
San Francisco, San Francisco State Univ. (415) 338-1664

Chico, Cal. State Univ. (916) 898-6485

Fresno, Cal. State Univ. (209) 278-3277

Saratoga, West Valley Coll. (408) 867-2200 x5601

Oakland, Mills Coll. (415) 430-2080

Martinez, Golden Eagle Parent Committee (Title V) (415) 372-0547

Long Beach, California State Univ (213) 985-5293

MAY
Stanford Univ. (415) 723-4078

Cupertino, De Anza Coll. (408) 973-9085

Susanville, Mother's Day Intertribal (916) 257-5222

Casa de Fruta, Santa Cruz Indian Council (408) 459-7929

JUNE
Oakland, Intertribal (415) 452-1235

Tehachapi, Indian Hills (209) 268-3228

Carson City, NV, Stewart Indian Museum (702) 882-1808

JULY
Santa Ynez Reservation, July 4th Powwow (805) 688-7997

Manteca, Three Rivers Lodge, July 4th Powwow (209) 858-2421

AUGUST
Costa Mesa, Orange Co. Fairgrounds, S. Cal. Ind. Centers (714) 530-0221

SEPTEMBER
Stockton, Edison High School (Title V) and Cent. Calif. Ind. Council (Labor Day) (209) 944-4803

San Jose, Indian Youth Council (408) 971-9622

CALIFORNIA INDIAN DAYS
Roseville (916) 920-0285

Barona Reservation (619) 281-5964

Colorado River Reservation (602) 669-9211

Ft. Yuma Reservation (619) 572-0213

OCTOBER
Ft. Mojave Reservation (619) 326-4591

Carson City, NV, Washoe Community (702) 885-9759

NOVEMBER
Kernville, Kern Valley Council (P.O. Box 169, Kernville, CA 93230)

DECEMBER
San Jose, Santa Clara Indian Center (408) 971-9622

SOUTHERN CALIFORNIA
Monthly scheduled events: (Other unscheduled powwows are held throughout the year in Southern California. Please consult your local Indian Center for a monthly calendar.)

1st SATURDAY OF EACH MONTH
Eagle Rock Recreation Center
(or other locations), Los Angeles Sponsor: Little Big Horn Club

2nd SATURDAY OF EACH MONTH
Cecil B. DeMille Jr. High School,
Long Beach, Los Angeles Co.
Sponsor: Many Trails Club (213) 371-2026 or 372-1842

3rd SATURDAY OF EACH MONTH
Eagle Rock Recreation Center, Los Angeles Co. Sponsor: LACCIM
(Los Angeles Co. Concerned Indian Movement) (818) 575-3512

4th SATURDAY OF EACH MONTH
Stanton Community Ctr., Stanton (nr. Anaheim), Orange Co. Sponsor: Orange Co. Indian Center (Garden Grove) (714) 530-0221

NORTHERN CALIFORNIA
(For a complete listing of these and unscheduled powwows, write the Intertribal Friendship House, 523 E. 14th St., Oakland, CA 94606 for their annual calendar.)

ALMOST MONTHLY
D-Q University, Davis, Yolo Co.
Sponsor: D-Q U (916) 758-1470

CALIFORNIA MISSIONS 1769-1834

APPENDIX B

The missions listed below are the original Roman Catholic "Chain of 21" and their asistencias (auxilliaries). The Native peoples from whom the missions were drawn are given in italics. With the exception of Pala, none exist today on reservations. Of course, other Catholic and Protestant churches are present on many reservations today. (The listing is south to north; numbers in boldface type refer to California Historical Landmarks.)

1769 San Diego de Alcalá (**242, 52**) Indian name: Nipaguay
Tipai, Ipai, Kameyaay (all formerly called *Diegueño*)

1780 La Purísima Concepción (**350**) (orig. site destroyed 1781)
Quechan (formerly called *Yuman*), *Cócopa*

1818 Asistencia de Santa Ysabel (**369**) Indian name: Elenaman
Ipai, Tipai, Cupeño, Cahuilla, Luiseño (?)

1798 San Luís Rey de Francia (**239**)
Luiseño, Gabrielino

1816 Asistencia de San António de Pala (**243**)
Luiseño, Cupeño, Cahuilla

1823 Asistencia Las Flores (**616**)
Luiseño, Juaneño

1776 San Juan Capistrano (**200**)
Luiseño, Juaneño, Gabrielino (?)

1830 Asistencia de San Bernardino (**42**) and the Zanja (waterworks) (**43**) Indian name: Guachama
Gabrielino, Cahuilla, Serrano

1771 San Gabriel Arcángel (**158**)
Gabrielino, Serrano, probably *Tataviam* and *Vanyume*

1797 San Fernando Rey de España (**157**)
Gabrielino (Fernandeño), Chumash, Tataviam, Kawaiisu

1782 San Buenaventura (**310**)
Chumash, Kawaiisu, Yokuts (?)

1786 Santa Bárbara Virgen y Martir (**309**)
Chumash (formerly called *Canalino*)

1804 Santa Ynéz (or Inés) (**305**)
Chumash

1787 La Purísima Concepción (**340**) (2nd site)
Chumash

1772 San Luis Obispo de Tolosa (**325**)
Chumash, Yokuts

1831 Asistencia de Santa Margarita (**364**)
Chumash

1797 San Miguel Arcángel (**326**)
Salinan

1771 San António de Pádua (**232**)
Salinan, Yokuts, Esselen

1791 Nuestra Señora de Soledad (**233**)
Salinan, Yokuts, Esselen, Costanoan

1770 San Carlos Borromeo del Rio Carmelo (Carmel) (**135**)
Esselen and *Costanoan* (mostly *Rumsen*)

1797 San Juan Bautista (**195**)
Costanoan (mostly *Mutsun*), *Yokuts*

1791 Exaltación de la Santa Cruz (**342**)
Costanoan groups

1791 Santa Clara de Asís (**250**)
1st site, Indian name: Soco-is-uka, and (**338**)
2nd site, Indian name: Gerguensun
Costanoan, Yokuts, Plains Miwok

1797 Gloriosísima Patriarca Señor José (**334**)
Costanoan (Ohlone), Yokuts,
also *Plains, Lake* and *Coast Miwok*

1776 San Francisco de Asís (Dolores) (**327**)
Costanoan groups, *Miwok, Patwin*

1817 San Rafael Arcángel (**220**)
Coast Miwok

1823 San Franscisco Solano (**3**)
Coast Miwok, Patwin (Suisun), Wappo

▲ *Colbert Eyraud, curator of* Cabot's Old Indian Pueblo,
*a relatively recently constructed museum in Desert Hot Springs.
The museum is a repository for numerous Indian artifacts collected
around the Southwest.*

MUSEUMS & CULTURAL CENTERS

APPENDIX C

Selected for their special treatment of California Indians. For a complete listing, see *Earth Is Our Mother: A Guide to the Indians of California*, Appendix D, California Museums with Indian Artifacts, p. 172. Readers who intend a visit to any of the regions of California Indian Country are strongly advised to first visit a local museum or one of the larger museums or cultural centers in order to get a good orientation on the Native traditions.

🖎 indicates museums with Indian dioramas.

EASTERN AND SOUTHERN CALIFORNIA

 ANTELOPE VALLEY (Los Angeles Co.) Antelope Valley (State) Indian Museum. *Kitanemuk, Paiute, Shoshone*

BANNING Malki Museum.
Cahuilla, Luiseño, Gabrielino, Serrano, Ipai, Tipai, Cupa, Chemehuevi, Chumash, Mohave, Yuman

BORREGO SPRINGS Anza-Borrego State Park Visitor Center. *Cahuilla, Ipai-Tipai, Yaqui*

 DEATH VALLEY NATIONAL MONUMENT.
Shoshone

DESERT HOT SPRINGS Cabot's Old Indian Pueblo Museum. (Not a pueblo) *Cahuilla, others*

FORT TEJON Fort Tejon State Historic Park. (Typical army Indian War fort). *Kawaiisu, Tubatubal, others*

FORT YUMA Ft. Yuma Reservation Museum.
Quechan, other Colorado River peoples

INDEPENDENCE Eastern California Museum.
Paiute, Shoshone, Washo

LAKE PERRIS Ya'I Heki', Home of the Wind Regional Indian Museum. (State Park) *Luiseño, Juaneño, Cahuilla, other desert peoples.*

LOS ANGELES
Natural History Museum.
All-California and Southwestern peoples

University of California Museum of Cultural History.
All California, others

PALM SPRINGS Desert Museum.
SW & California desert

PASADENA Southwest Museum.
All-California, North America

 OJAI Ojai Valley Museum.
Chumash

RANDSBURG Desert Museum.
Coso Shoshone, Paiute, Mohave, Kawaiisu

REDLANDS San Bernardino County Museum and San Gabriel Asistencia. *All California, others*

RIDGECREST-CHINA LAKE Maturango Museum.
Coso and Panamint Shoshone, Yokuts

RIVERSIDE Riverside Municipal Museum.
Serrano, Luiseño, Cahuilla, other California

 SAN DIEGO San Diego Museum of Man.
Southern and All-California, others

 SANTA ANA Bowers Museum.
Southern California, other Southwestern peoples

TWENTYNINE PALMS Joshua Tree National Monument Visitor Center.
Serrano, Cahuilla, Chemehuevi

YUCAIPA Mousley Museum of Natural History.
Serrano, Cahuilla, Luiseño, Mohave, California, U.S.

MUSEUMS & CULTURAL CENTERS, continued

CENTRAL CALIFORNIA

 BAKERSFIELD Kern County Museum.
Yokuts, others

BERKELEY Lowie Museum of Anthropology,
University of California.
All California, North America

FREMONT Coyote Hills Regional Park.
Ohlone (Costanoan), Miwok

FRESNO The Discovery Center.
Yokuts, other California, Plains, and Southwestern peoples

LAKEPORT Lake County Museum.
Pomo, Wappo, Lake Miwok

LODI San Joaquin County Historical Museum.
California, others

LOMPOC La Purísima Mission State Historic Park.
(Typical mission) *Chumash, other California*

MONTEREY Monterey Bay Aquarium.
Ohlone & Rumsen Costanoan

 MORRO BAY Morro Bay State Park Museum of Natural
History. *Chumash*

 NORTH FORK Sierra Mono Museum.
Monache, Paiute, Yokuts, Sierra Foothills

NOVATO Marin Museum of the American Indian.
Miwok, other California peoples

 OAKLAND Oakland Museum.
Pomo, Ohlone (Costanoan)

PETALUMA Petaluma Adobe State Historic Park.
(Spanish Rancho) *Miwok, Patwin, Wappo*

PINE GROVE-JACKSON Chaw-Se Indian Grinding
Rocks State Park. *Miwok*

POINT REYES NATIONAL SEASHORE
Visitor Center. *Central Coastal California*

 REDDING Redding Museum and Art Center.
California and other U.S.

 SACRAMENTO State Indian Museum.
All California

 SAN FRANCISCO California Academy of Sciences.
All-Native American

 SANTA BARBARA Santa Barbara Museum of Natural
History. *Chumash, California, others*

SANTA ROSA Jesse Peter Memorial Museum.
Pomo, other Central California

STOCKTON Pioneer Museum and Haggin Galleries.
Miwok, Washo, Pomo, others

UKIAH Grace Hudson Sun House Museum.
Pomo, Yuki

WILLETS Mendocino County Museum.
Pomo, Yuki

 YOSEMITE NATIONAL PARK.
Miwok, Shoshone, Paiute, Monache, Washo, Yokuts

NORTHERN CALIFORNIA

 EUREKA Clarke Memorial Museum.
Karok, Yurok, Hupa, Pomo

—Fort Humboldt State Historic Park.
Karok, Yurok, Hupa

FALL RIVER MILLS Ft. Crook Museum.
Pit River Tribes, Modoc

HOOPA Hupa Reservation Museum.
Hupa and surrounding peoples

LAKE OROVILLE Visitor Center.
Maidu

TULELAKE Lava Beds National Monument.
Modoc, Klamath, Pit River Tribes

WEAVERVILLE
Trinity County Historical Society-
J.J. Jackson Memorial Museum.
Shasta, Chimariko, Wintu, Lassik, Wailaki, Yuki

ARCHAEOLOGICAL AND VILLAGE SITES

APPENDIX D

These are sites that have been protected to some extent. Although hundreds of other sites exist, they are essentially unprotected, and the reader will forgive me for not listing them. (Listed north to south.)

Lava Beds National Park Siskiyou Co. Red and yellow pictographs (rock paintings) in lava caves. Modoc petroglyphs (rock carvings) at various sites (enquire of ranger).

Fort Jones Museum Siskiyou Co. Rain rock (with rounded pits) used by Shasta shamans for invoking weather changes and for fertility.

Patricks Point State Park Del Norte Co. Reconstructed Yurok village of Sumeg. Used for ceremonies.

Hoopa Valley Reservation Humboldt Co. Several restored ancient Hupa village sites, some 5,000 years old, used for ceremonies.

Chaw-Se, Indian Grinding Rocks State Historic Park Amador Co. Petroglyphs and grinding rocks. Museum.

Coyote Hills Regional Park Alameda Co. A cross-section of a midden and a reconstructed Ohlone village. Museum.

Presidio of Monterey Museum Monterey Co. Rain or "baby" rock, similar to that at Fort Jones.

Kule Loklo, Point Reyes National Seashore Marin Co. A reconstructed Coast Miwok village (see p. 53). Used for ceremonies.

Yosemite National Park, Sequoia-Kings Canyon National Park Several petroglyph sites — ask a ranger and visit the Visitors Centers. Reconstructed Sierra Miwok and Shoshone village at Yosemite used for ceremonies.

Chumash Painted Cave Santa Barbara Co. Ancient ceremonial Chumash site with brightly-painted pictographs.

Tule River Reservation Tulare Co. Painted Cave. Huge multicolored paintings of fantastic animals and spirits. Grinding rocks. Guided tour only, see tribal office.

Coso Shoshone Petroglyphs San Bernardino Co. (Arrangements must be made at Maturango Museum, Ridgecrest, or Desert Museum, Randsburg, as the sites are on a Naval weapons testing area.)

Rock Maze San Bernardino Co. Ancient furrowed field of religious importance (see p. 116).

No person may excavate, remove, damage, or otherwise alter of deface any archaeological resource located on public lands or Indian lands... Penalties of up to $20,000 fine and 2 years imprisonment for violation are provided and have been levied.

Giant Desert Intaglios Riverside Co. Huge spirit figures carved in the desert pavement (see p. 114).

Fish Traps Riverside Co. 10,000-year-old fishing method on ancient Lake Cahuilla (see p. 19).

Hemet Maze Stone Riverside Co. Small amazing carving of a labyrinth.

Calico Early Man Site San Bernardino Co. One of the oldest known Indian sites in North America. See digs in progress.

Joshua Tree National Monument Riverside Co. Several fertility pictographs. See park interpretive center.

Anza-Borrego Desert State Park San Diego Co. Petroglyphs at Little Pass Campground.

Roundhouses (Dancehouses) may be seen at the following locations. Roundhouses must never be entered without permission; many are privately owned.

Ahwahnee Village (Yosemite Park)

Big Valley Rancheria (Private)

Chaw-Se Indian Grinding Rocks State Park

Colusa Rancheria

Grindstone Creek Rancheria

Janesville (Private)

Laytonville Rancheria

Manchester Rancheria

Kule Loklo (Point Reyes National Seashore)

Stewarts Point (Kashaya) Rancheria (Private)

Tuolumne Rancheria

Wassama Roundhouse (town of Ahwahnee)

West Point (Private)

Pa-che-pus (Esselen Ranch)

TRADERS, SHOWS AND CRAFTS SHOPS

APPENDIX E
WHERE TO FIND GENUINE INDIAN ARTS & CRAFTS.

Collecting, owning, and wearing Indian artwork are popular undertakings of thousands, if not millions, of Americans. These works of art or artisanship are popular primarily because of their real, intrinsic beauty, but also partly because of their direct connection to the Native American, and partly because of a desire to aid a group of deserving, less fortunate persons.

To find the genuine articles, I will give some rather general directions, and a few specific ones. First, I recommend one or several visits to larger powwows and Indian gatherings. Very few such festivals are without a number of crafts booths. In addition to well-made traditional items, some daringly new things seem to show up, if you spend the time looking.

Second, Indian fairs, markets, and trade shows are the places to find the more unusual things, bulkier and more fragile pieces (like ceramics and weavings), and especially, antiques. Not all fairs are run by Indians, however, and the selling of an antique never profits its creator.

Third, shops can be found as "trading posts," stores featuring Indian arts & crafts, museum shops, reservation arts & crafts shops, and individual artist's shops.

In the past, *caveat emptor* (let the buyer beware) was the word on genuineness; however, since the Indian Arts and Crafts Act of 1990, let the seller beware has spawned a lot of problems for some Indians. The law was intended to protect Indian sellers from non-Indian copies, forgeries, imports, and imitations, but the seller has had to possess a documentation of Indianness, frequently more difficult to obtain than that from the BIA.

As the reader will understand from the text, many Natives never had a reservation to belong to, many others have never chosen to affiliate with a tribe, and others have come to California from afar and have no easy way to determine their specific heritage. Therefore, buyers may find articles labelled something like: "not guaranteed to be Indian, as defined by law." Changes to the law to make it more fair may be in the works.

ARTS & CRAFTS GALLERIES
(a selected few, some Indian-owned, some not)

Trinidad Trading Co.
460 Main St., Trinidad, CA 95570

Indian Arts Gift Shop
241 F St., Eureka, CA 95501

Bear n' Coyote Gallery
Jamestown, CA 95327

Pacific Western Traders
305 Wool St., Folsom, CA 95630

Gallery of the American West
121 K St., Sacramento, CA 95814

Southwesterly
698 Mason, San Francisco, CA 94108

American Indian Contemporary Arts Gallery
685 Market St., San Francisco, CA 94105-4212

Reyna's Gallerias
106 Third St., San Juan Bautista, CA 95045

Ojai Indian Shop
318 E. Ojai Ave., Ojai, CA 93023

Buffalo Robe Indian Trading Post
8415 Reseda, Northridge, CA

Indian Art Center of California
12666 Ventura Blvd., Studio City, CA

Wounded Knee Indian Gallery
2313 Wilshire Blvd., Santa Monica CA 90403

American Indian Store
1095 S. Magnolia, El Cajon, CA 92020

See also goods for sale at your local
American Indian Center: Sacramento, Los Angeles.

MUSEUM SHOPS
(a highly subjective list; your suggestions are invited):

Yosemite National Park. Ansel Adams Gallery & Ahwahnee Lodge.

Southwest Museum, Pasadena. Native American artwork and craftwork from the hemisphere.

Museum of Man, San Diego. Worldwide things.

RESERVATION SHOPS
(smaller, but definitely authentic):

Hoopa Museum

Pomo Museum (Lake Mendocino)

Ya-ka-ama (Education Center)

Tule River (silversmiths)

Bishop (Paiute-Shoshone Cultural Center)

Fort Mojave, Chemehuevi, Colorado Tribes (at their museums)

Morongo (Malki Museum)

Agua Caliente (Palm Springs Trading Post).

TRADERS

The magazine *Indian Trader*, publication of the Indian Arts & Crafts Association, lists numerous trade shows here in California (as well as the West, in general). 311 E. Aztec Ave., Gallup, NM 87305.

The **American Indian Traders Guild** of Fresno presents trade shows and authenticates items by exhibitors (North America only). Membership Directory available. 3876 E. Tedora Ave., Fresno, CA 93762

The *American Indian Index*, from Denver, in 1985 listed 175 California outlets that sell Indian goods, including many trading posts, museum shops, and reservation shops. Arrowstar Publishing, 10134 University Park Station, Denver, CO 80210-0134.

BIBLIOGRAPHY
AND FURTHER READING

1. California Department of Parks and Recreation, William P. Mott, Director, *California Historical Landmarks*, 1973, and later editions. Contains the wording and locations of the bronze plaques around the state.

2. Cook, Sherburne F. *The Conflict Between the California Indian and White Civilization.* University of California Press, Berkeley, 1976. The facts and figures of the California Indian holocaust.

3. d'Angulo, Jaime, *Indian Tales.* Hill and Wang, New York, 1953 and later editions. Stories from the early 1900s of and by (mostly California) Indians. Several tapes are available from Heyday Books, Berkeley.

4. Eargle, Dolan H., *The Earth Is Our Mother: A Guide to the Indians of California, Their Locales & Historic Sites.* Trees Co. Press, San Francisco, 4th Ed.,1991. A history and detailed guidebook to all contemporary Indian places.

5. Forbes, Jack D., *Native Americans of California and Nevada.* Naturegraph Publishers, Happy Camp, CA, 1969 and later editions. A history of the peoples, with emphasis on Native languages and teaching of Indian history.

6. Heizer, Robert F., and Clewlow, C. W., *Prehistoric Rock Art of California* (2 vols.). Ballena Press, Menlo Park, CA, 1973.

7. Heizer, Robert F., and Elsasser, Albert B., *The Natural World of the California Indians.* University of California Press, 1980. An ethnological survey of the environment and traditions of the early peoples.

8. Heizer, Robert F., and Whipple, M. A., *The California Indians, A Source Book.* University of California Press, Berkeley, 2nd Ed., 1971. A compilation of writings about the original California Indians.

9. Kroeber, Alfred L., *Handbook of the Indians of California.* Orig. *Bureau of American Ethnology Bulletin (78)*, reprinted by University of California Press, Berkeley. The first compiled, detailed description of the peoples of central California.

10. Kroeber, Theodora, *Ishi in Two Worlds.* University of California Press, Berkeley, 1971. The true story of Ishi, a Yahi-Yana man of the Sierra forests, forced to surrender after years of persecution in the forests.

11. Margolin, Malcolm, Publisher, *News From Native California.* Heyday Books, Berkeley, CA. A quarterly periodical that informs all aspects of the past and present. An indispensible publication for everyone interested in the California Indian people.

12. Margolin, Malcolm, *The Ohlone Way.* Heyday Books, Berkeley, 1978. Descriptions of the modes of living of many coastal and riverine California cultures; applicable to many other peoples, this is about the Ohlone (Costanoans) of central California.

13. Margolin, Malcolm, *The Way We Lived.* Heyday Books, Berkeley, 1982. Deeply moving short stories of and by Native people of California. Anyone wishing to know the spirit of California Indians must read this book.

14. Martineau, LeVan, *The Rocks Begin to Speak.* KC Publications, Las Vegas, 1973 and later editions. This book moves rock art from the ambiguous or mysterious to communicative art with meaning.

15. Rawls, James D., *Indians of California, The Changing Image*, University of Oklahoma Press, Norman, OK, 1984. Rawls cites Stephen Powers, 1872: "Men damn what they do not understand." It is Rawls' purpose here to make us understand.

16. Sturtevant, William C., General Editor, *Handbook of North American Indians.* Vol. 8 (1978), *California*, Robert F. Heizer, Editor; Vol. 9 (1979), *Southwest*, Alfonso Ortiz, Editor; Vol. 10 (1983), *Southwest*, Alfonso Ortiz, Editor; Vol. 11 (1986), *Great Basin*, Warren L. d'Azevedo, Editor. Smithsonian Institution, Washington, D.C. These are the primary references for the history of Native America, in which detailed information and references are given on every known group.

Several publishers have an interest in specific tribes or aspects of California Indians. We present a listing of the publishers, so that the reader may write for their catalogs.

Ballena Press, 833 Valparaiso, Menlo Park, CA 94025

Capra Press, Box 2068, Santa Barbara, CA 93120

Heyday Books, Box 9145, Berkeley, CA 94709

Malki Museum Press, Morongo Reservation, Banning, CA 92220

Naturegraph Publishers, 3543 Indian Creek Rd., Happy Camp, CA 96039

Stanford University Press, Stanford, CA 94305

University of California Press, 2120 Berkeley Way, Berkeley, CA 94720

University of California, Los Angeles, American Indian Studies Center, 3220 Campbell Hall, Los Angeles, CA 90024

Westernlore Press, 11860 Pami Pl., Tucson, AZ 85704

Yosemite Natural History Association, Box 230, El Portal, CA 95318

Persons who wish to become aware of new developments among California, other United States tribal groups, and tribal groups in other countries will want reference to further informational sources. These include:

News From Native California. This is a quarterly publication focussing on California peoples, which features articles on history, language, legal aspects, education, health, events, news, and just about every other topic of Indian interest. Published by Heyday Press, P.O. Box 9145, Berkeley, CA 94709 ($17.16/yr.)

International Indian Treaty Council (IITC). The IITC, though based in California, is truly an international sentinel, which investigates, documents, and publicizes offenses against the rights of tribal or indigenous people anywhere in the hemisphere, indeed on other continents, as well. Write for their bulletin. IITC, 710 Clayton St., San Francisco, CA 94117.

South (and Central) American Indian Information Center (SAIIC). The center furnishes news, articles, and information on numerous indigenous peoples south of the United States. SAIIC also sponsors a number of informative meetings, lectures, and gatherings in various cities in California. SAIIC, 1212 Broadway, Oakland, CA 94612.

American Indian Centers are to be found in the larger cities of California. Several of these centers publish calendars of events of interest to their local constituents. Many of these centers also sponsor other programs of education, powwows, and lectures, as well as supervising the disbursement of health, head start education, and welfare benefits to urban Indian dwellers. [Other names used are Native American Indian Centers or Intertribal Centers, and occasionally information may be obtained from Bureau of Indian Affairs offices-U.S. Department of the Interior.)

INDEX